Elements of Literature®

W9-AUO-075

Holt English Language Development

An ESL/ESOL Guide for Newcomers

HOLT, RINEHART AND WINSTON

ISBN 978-0-55-401087-8

ISBN 0-55-401087-9

2 3 4 5 179 12 11 10 09 08

Guide to English for Newcomers

The Guide to English for Newcomers familiarizes students with the basic grammar, survival vocabulary, and language they need to obtain necessities, make requests, and understand instructions. The guide consists of 20 lessons, all of which incorporate listening, speaking, reading, and writing. As building a strong foundation is essential to a student's subsequent progress, the lessons begin with close student-teacher interaction, and later allow for monitored paired or independent student activities.

In addition to presenting attainable goals for beginners, the guide bridges the gap between students' daily life and classroom material. When students associate English with their personal experiences, they retain more vocabulary and grammar. Consequently, each lesson is organized around a theme, such as *Activities in the Classroom, In Case of Emergency,* or *What Happened Last Weekend?* This, along with the numerous speaking, writing, and reading opportunities in each lesson, ensures that each student interacts with both lesson content and with his or her peers and teacher, resulting in effective lessons that promote acquisition within a limited time frame.

EACH LESSON CONTAINS

- A detailed lesson plan with prompts and tips for the instructor
- Word drills to ensure proper pronunciation
- A Language Blast for fast acquisition of Tier I vocabulary
- An array of worksheets to focus on Tier I vocabulary, other lesson vocabulary, lesson grammar, and reading and listening comprehension
- Paired speaking exercises simulating real-life situations
- Grammar and vocabulary reinforcement activities allowing for student response
- A reading application to promote independent practice of the lesson material

PROGRAM OVERVIEW

Lesson Theme	Language Blast	Grammar Point	Lesson Vocabulary
1. Introductions	Cardinal Numbers	Present Tense *be* with Subjects and Subject Pronouns	student, teacher, friend, class, teammate, coach, artist, musician, athlete, cook, girl, boy
2. Personal Information	Money	Present Tense *be* with Interrogative Sentences	name, city, state, birth date, street, address, phone number, favorite food, favorite book, favorite movie
3. Daily Routines	Seasons	Present Tense Verbs with Subject/Verb Agreement	wake up, get up, brush hair/teeth, take a shower, eat breakfast, go to school, go to class, eat lunch, go home, do homework, play sports, practice an instrument, eat dinner, watch TV, go to sleep
4. Classroom Objects and Supplies / Activities in the Classroom	Days of the Week	Present Tense *do* with Interrogative Sentences	desk, board, clock, computer, map, chair, ruler, eraser, pencil, paper, textbook, notebook, pass tests, ask questions, finish homework, solve problems, take notes, teach lessons, help classmates
5. In Case of Emergency	Review Daily Routine Vocabulary	Imperative	Go to the doctor, call the police, call for help, police officer, paramedic, firefighter, nurse, hospital, police station, bandage, earthquake, fire, flood
6. Activities with Friends	Months of the Year	Present Progressive	playing a game, reading a book, listening to music, singing a song, eating a meal, walking to school, going out, watching a movie, talking on the phone
7. What Are You Doing?	Review Days of the Week and Months of the Year	Present Progressive *to be + subject + gerund* in Interrogative Sentences	Questions words – Who? What? When? Where? Why? How? plus gerunds from last lesson
8. Types of Classes	Parts of the Body	Possessive Nouns	language arts, math, physical education, social studies, homeroom, chemistry, art, music, science, biology, history, hair, head, shoulders, neck, throat, back, chest, stomach, arms, elbows, hands, wrists, fingers, legs, knees, ankles, feet, toes, face, ears, nose, eyes, mouth, tongue, cheeks, eyebrows, teeth, lips
9. Physical Characteristics	Ordinal Numbers	Adjectives	big, clean, dirty, small, long, short, tall, fat, thin, ugly, pretty
10. Comparing Places Inside a School	Adjectives	Regular Comparatives and Superlatives	reinforce adjectives from previous lesson and auditorium, gym, library, cafeteria, hallway, classroom, locker, office

Lesson Theme	Language Blast	Grammar Point	Lesson Vocabulary
11. Describing Yourself and Others	Adjectives	Regular Comparatives and Superlatives	intelligent, stupid, interesting, dull, funny, talkative, nervous, energetic, hopeful, elegant, frightened, playful, loving
12. Plans for the Weekend	Comparatives and Superlatives	Simple Future Tense *going to*	going to see, going to go, going to dance, going to study, going to go shopping, mall, club, a friend's house, downtown, the beach
13. Life Predictions and Spontaneous Decisions	Comparatives and Superlatives	Simple Future *will*	I think I will…Have kids, get married, be a (doctor), go to college, buy a house/ apartment, live in (California), have a family, get a job, live in a different country, travel around the world, start my own business, write a book, direct a movie, be on TV
14. Lost in the City	Prepositions of Place	Prepositions of Place	bank, post office, restaurant, museum, stadium, hospital, train station, library, supermarket, café, bus stop, hotel in, on, at, over, under, behind, around the corner in front of, beside, to the left, to the right, across from
15. Chores / Preparing for an Exam	Prepositions of Place	*Have to* and *need to* Phrases	clean the room, sweep the floor, take out the trash, make the bed, dust the furniture, vacuum the carpet, study, read, review, practice
16. Time	Time	Past Tense Regular and Irregular	talk, say, think, do, make, see, and practice prepositions of place (in, on, at)
17. Don't Be Late!	Past Tense Verbs	Past tense *had to* and *needed to*	practice making excuses with verbs that have already been covered, especially past tense of *have to* and *need to*
18. Food and Drink	Irregular *to be* and *to have*	Past Tense Regular and Irregular	vegetables (carrot, broccoli, potato, tomato, pepper, lettuce, cucumber, onion), fruit (apple, pear, orange, watermelon, kiwi, cantaloupe, grape, blueberry, strawberry), chicken, fish, beef, ham, rice, cheese, pasta, sandwich, bread, soup, water, juice, soda, coffee, tea
19. What Happened Last Weekend?	Irregular Past Tense Verbs	Past Tense Irregular	begin, become, bring, buy, eat, drink, fall, feel, forget, fly, get, give, go, hear, know, meet, make, pay, read, run, send, say, see, take, teach, take, think, throw, understand, win, write
20. Place Settings/ At a Party	Irregular Past Tense Verbs	Modal Verbs	plate, cup, napkin, spoon, fork, knife, bowl, glass, and continue with verbs

Table of Contents

Holt English Language Development

Guide to English for Newcomers

Lesson 1: Introductions

STEP 1: WORD DRILL *3 MINUTES*
(Teach/Guided Practice) Greet the class, and wave while saying, *Hello!* Gesture to the class to repeat: *Hello*. After class has repeated, say *Hello* again and elicit a second repetition. This establishes a rhythm that used to introduce new or difficult words: teacher first and then the class.

(Guided Practice) After students have echoed as a class, point to random individual students, say hello, and invite the student to repeat alone. This routine should always be used when introducing new words in order to keep the students involved. It ensures that the words are being pronounced correctly by everybody.

STEP 2: BUILD BACKGROUND *10 MINUTES*
(Teach/Guided Practice/Practice) This is a continuation of Step 1 and can be used as a way of introducing yourself. Write the short dialogue below on the board, read the first two lines aloud, and elicit repetition from the students after each line.

Let each student practice introducing him or herself, starting the dialogue from the beginning each time. After each student has had a turn, continue with the remaining four lines of the dialogue. Repeat until students are comfortable pronouncing the words. Then say the first line (A), and elicit the class to respond (B). Reverse roles. When results are satisfactory, allow students to practice the new routine in pairs while teacher circulates and monitors progress.

A: Hello! I am _____. What is your name?

B: Hello! I am _____.

A: How are you?

B: I'm fine, thanks. How are you?

A: I'm fine, thanks. It is nice to meet you.

B: It is nice to meet you too.

STEP 3: INDEPENDENT RECITATION *4 MINUTES*
(Apply) If students grasp Step 2 quickly, give them two minutes to memorize the dialogue on the board. When time is up, erase the dialogue and chose a few pairs to recite it from memory.

STEP 4: LANGUAGE BLAST *15 MINUTES*
(Teach/Guided Practice/Practice) Ask students how high they can count in English. Start with one and count until the students have stopped. Work on pronunciation and drill difficult numbers. After students can count to fifty as a class, go around the room, pointing to individual students until each student has said a number. Pass out Worksheet 1.1 and allow students 5-10 minutes to complete it.

LESSON OBJECTIVES
Students will:
- respond to basic questions used in a greeting
- learn plural and describe themselves and their peers
- speak in complete, coherent sentences to make introductions
- use declarative sentences to identify peers and describe themselves
- listen to instructions and to their peers' dialogue

LESSON VOCABULARY
student, teacher, friend, class, teammate, coach, artist, musician, athlete, cook, girl, boy

LESSON RESOURCES
Worksheet 1.1
Language Blast: Numerals and Words, Cardinal Numbers

Worksheet 1.2
Vocabulary Development: People We Know

Worksheet 1.3
Speaking and Listening: Plural Nouns

Worksheet 1.4
Reading and Fluency

Worksheet 1.5
Daily Review

Teaching Tip The word *drill* is highly effective when the teacher generates a high energy level using as many gestures as possible, and elicits constant responses and participation from the class.

STEP 5: VOCABULARY DEVELOPMENT *10 MINUTES*

(Teach/Practice/Apply) Distribute a copy of Worksheet 1.2 to each student. Begin by asking the students if they recognize any of the vocabulary next to the pictures. Point to each picture and pronounce the word next to it. Invite the class to repeat the vocabulary in unison. Then ask students to practice it in pairs. Monitor the students' interaction and intervene if any incorrect pronunciation is overheard.

STEP 6: GRAMMAR AND CONVENTIONS *8 MINUTES*

(Guided Practice) Ask the class: *What change do we make to a noun if there is more than one? Say you have one friend, what do you add to* friend *to make it plural?* Help students answer: *We add an –s when there is more than one friend.*

Now ask: *What change do we make to a noun plural that ends in* y *or* ch? Help students answer: *We add an –es to nouns that end in* ch. *We add an –ies to nouns that end in* y. Distribute a copy of Worksheet 1.3 to each student to practice forming plural nouns. Have students complete the first half of the worksheet.

SPEAKING AND LISTENING

(Practice/Apply) To reinforce introductions, as well as vocabulary comprehension, allow students to complete the second half of Worksheet 1.3 in pairs. Monitor activity and correct any grammar or pronunciation errors. Correct in class or collect when the lesson is finished.

STEP 7: READING AND FLUENCY *10 MINUTES*

(Apply/Review) Distribute a copy of Worksheet 1.4 to each student. If time allows, choose a few students to read the selection aloud. If not, students should read it independently and answer the follow-up questions in the second part of the worksheet. Correct in class or collect when the lesson is finished.

Optional Memory Game 10-15 minutes
Photocopy the Memory Game on page 150 (make 1-3 copies depending on class size), and cut out individual sentences. Make sure students feel comfortable pronouncing the vocabulary before starting. Distribute one sentence to each student. Start at one corner of the room, asking the student to read his or her sentence aloud to the class: *I am a girl.* Now the teacher should repeat *She is a girl.* and then add his or her own sentence: *I am a teacher.* Teacher then invites the next student to follow the pattern: *She is a girl. He is a teacher.* and *I am a teammate.* This continues until every student has taken a turn. Anybody who needs more than one clue to complete his or her turn is out.

Worksheet 1.4 Note
In this activity students will encounter unfamiliar words. If their meaning cannot be immediately extrapolated from the text, guide students though a reasoning process that leads to a better understanding of the selection instead of directly feeding them the definition. You can also ask the other students in the class if they have understood the word in question, and encourage those who have to assist their classmates.

Note: To allow for further review, Worksheet 1.5 may be assigned as homework.

Worksheet 1.1: Language Blast

Numerals and Words

DIRECTIONS Look at the numbers and study the words. Then complete the exercises below.

1 – one	11 – eleven	21 – twenty-one	40 – forty	500 – five hundred
2 – two	12 – twelve	22 – twenty-two	50 – fifty	600 – six hundred
3 – three	13 – thirteen	23 – twenty-three	60 – sixty	700 – seven hundred
4 – four	14 – fourteen	24 – twenty-four	70 – seventy	800 – eight hundred
5 – five	15 – fifteen	25 – twenty-five	80 – eighty	900 – nine hundred
6 – six	16 – sixteen	26 – twenty-six	90 – ninety	
7 – seven	17 – seventeen	27 – twenty-seven	100 – one hundred	
8 – eight	18 – eighteen	28 – twenty-eight	200 – two hundred	
9 – nine	19 – nineteen	29 – twenty-nine	300 – three hundred	
10 – ten	20 – twenty	30 – thirty	400 – four hundred	

1000 – one thousand

10,000 – ten thousand

100,000 – one hundred thousand

1,000,000 – one million

1,000,000,000 – one billion

1,100,900 – One million, one hundred thousand, nine hundred

498 – four hundred and ninety-eight

1,200 – One thousand two hundred

301,000 – Three hundred and one thousand

300,100 – Three hundred thousand one hundred

300,001 – Three hundred thousand and one

Cardinal Numbers

DIRECTIONS Change the words to numerals.

1. Nineteen _____ .

2. Forty-two _____ .

3. One thousand nine hundred and three _____ .

DIRECTIONS Change the numerals to words.

4. 89 _____ .

5. 313 _____ .

6. 3,600 _____ .

Worksheet 1.2: Vocabulary Development

People We Know

DIRECTIONS Look at the pictures and try to recognize the words you know. Listen as your teacher reads the vocabulary aloud, and pronounce the words with the rest of the class. Find a partner and practice pronouncing the words.

Worksheet 1.3: Speaking and Listening

Plural Nouns

DIRECTIONS In English, plural nouns are made by adding *-s, –es,* or *–ies*.
With a partner, change the singular nouns below to plural.

1. athlete _____

2. teammate _____

3. musician _____

4. coach _____

5. artist _____

6. friend _____

7. cook _____

8. teacher _____

9. girl _____

10. lady _____

11. boy _____

12. baby _____

Dialogue

DIRECTIONS Read the dialogue with your partner. Use your own names and
the vocabulary words from the list above. Check each vocabulary word as you
use it. Use at least 10 words.

A: Hello. My name is _____.

B: Hi. I'm _____.

A: It is nice to meet you.

B: It is nice to meet you, too.

A: Are you a _____?

B: No, I am not a _____. I am a student.

A: Welcome to our class.

B: Thank you!

Worksheet 1.4: Reading and Fluency

Reading for Understanding

DIRECTIONS Read the story below and use it to help you with the exercise in second part of the worksheet.

Opposites

DIRECTIONS Circle the sentences that best describe Tom and Anita. Then write the opposite of the sentences you do not circle in the space provided. The first one has been done for you.

1. They are brothers. _____.

2. They are teachers. _____.

3. They are students. _____.

4. They are coaches. _____.

5. They are friends. _____.

6. They are in the same class. _____.

7. Anita is a new student. _____.

Worksheet 1.5: Daily Review

Who Are You?

DIRECTIONS Check all the boxes next to the pictures that describe you. Then copy the complete sentence in the space below. For the boxes you do not check, write the opposite of the sentence next to the picture in the space below.

☐ I am an athlete.   ☐ I am a musician.   ☐ I am an artist.

_____.   _____.   _____.

Who Are They?

DIRECTIONS Look at each picture. Circle the sentence that best describes who each person is. In some cases, you must circle more than one sentence.

1. Who are the girls?
A. They are friends.
B. They are not teachers.

2. Who are the kids?
A. They are not artists.
B. They are musicians.

3. Who is Ms. Johnson?
   A. She is a friend.
   B. She is a coach.

Lesson 2: Personal Information

STEP 1: WORD DRILL *2 MINUTES*

(Teach/Guided Practice) Greet the class, and wave while saying: *Hello!* Gesture to the class to repeat: *Hello.* This establishes a rhythm that will be used to introduce new or difficult words: teacher first and then the class. After the class has repeated, *Hello!* say: *My name is ____.* Point to a student and ask: *What is your name?* Cue the student to answer by saying: *My name is _____.*

(Guided Practice) Continue to establish the pattern by repeating *My name is ____.* and pointing to a student and asking: *What is your name?* Cue the student to answer: *My name is _____.* Once the pattern is familiar, continue by having the student point to a classmate and ask: *What is your name?* Cue the next student answer: *My name is _____.* and point to another student, asking: *What is your name?* End exercise after each student has had a turn to ask and answer. Help students to ensure that the words are being pronounced correctly.

STEP 2: BUILD BACKGROUND *8 MINUTES*

(Teach/Guided Practice/Practice) This is a continuation of Step 1. Preteach the necessary vocabulary for the dialogue by using pictures, acting out words, or drawing items on the board. Write the short dialogue below on the board, read the first pair of lines aloud, and then point to random individual students, asking the question in line A and eliciting the correct response for line B. Repeat the dialogue until students are comfortable pronouncing the words.

Choose several students to ask you the questions in line A. Respond to their questions using text in line B. Next, divide students into pairs. Have each pair practice asking and answering the dialogue questions. Then have them switch roles. Allow students to practice the new routine while you circulate and monitor progress.

A: What is your name?

B: My name is _____.

A: Where do you live?

B: I live in the city of _____. I live in the state of _____.

A: What is your favorite food?

B: My favorite food is _____.

STEP 3: INDEPENDENT RECITATION *3 MINUTES*

(Apply) If students grasp Step 2 quickly, give them two minutes to memorize the dialogue on the board. When their time is up, erase the dialogue and ask students to recite it from memory in front of the class.

LESSON OBJECTIVES
Students will:

- respond with appropriate short phrases or sentences when asked personal information questions
- ask and answer personal information questions by using simple sentences and phrases
- learn how to use present tense verb *be* with interrogative sentences
- use interrogative sentences correctly to obtain information from peers
- listen to instructions and to their peers' dialogue

LESSON VOCABULARY
name, city, state, birth date, street, address, phone number, favorite food, favorite book, favorite movie

LESSON RESOURCES

Worksheet 2.1
Language Blast: Money

Worksheet 2.2
Vocabulary Development: Crossword Puzzle

Worksheet 2.3
Speaking and Listening: Classroom Survey

Worksheet 2.4
Reading and Fluency

Worksheet 2.5
Daily Review

Teaching Tip Using realia or pictures is a good way for students to quickly grasp the concepts of certain vocabulary items.

STEP 4: LANGUAGE BLAST *10 MINUTES*

(Teach/Guided Practice/Practice) Show students a penny. Ask them if they know how much it is worth. Repeat with a nickel, dime, quarter, and dollar bill. Help them with the correct pronunciation. Next, show different combinations, such as two quarters, and ask students how much you have (fifty cents). Take away one quarter and ask students how much you have left. (twenty-five cents). Repeat using different combinations of money. Pass out Worksheet 2.1 and read through it with students. Allow students 5-10 minutes to complete the worksheet.

STEP 5: VOCABULARY DEVELOPMENT *10 MINUTES*

(Teach/Practice/Apply) Distribute a copy of Worksheet 2.2 to each student. Read each item in the answer box and have students repeat after you. Ask students if they recognize any of the words. Teach any unfamiliar words using gestures and visuals. Check students' understanding by providing examples or eliciting them from the class. Model how to complete the crossword puzzle by completing the first clue with students. Read the clue for 1 Across with students. Point out the signal words *number* and *street*. Guide students to select the word *address* from the answer box. Point out the heading *Across* and the numeral 1 next to the clues. Find the numeral 1 on the puzzle board and trace your finger horizontally across the grid to model *across*. Write the word *address* in the appropriate boxes. Have students complete the crossword puzzle while you circulate and monitor progress.

STEP 6: GRAMMAR AND CONVENTIONS *15 MINUTES*

(Guided Practice) Say to the class: *My name is...* leaving the ending unfinished, as if you've forgotten. Say to class: *Now you ask, "What is your name?"* emphasizing the verb, *is*. After class repeats, answer: *My name is ___.* Repeat pattern using the following statements: *My birth date is..., My favorite food is..., My favorite book is..., My address is...* Ask several students to try leading the class, using the same pattern.

SPEAKING AND LISTENING

(Practice/Apply) Distribute a copy of Worksheet 2.3 to pairs of students. Ask them how well they think they know their classmates. Discuss the worksheet, and have students echo-read each question. Make sure students understand the vocabulary by providing examples or eliciting them. Allow pairs 5-7 minutes to ask each other questions to complete the exercise. Then ask questions to see what the students have learned. The students who questioned Mike must answer the question.

STEP 7: READING AND FLUENCY *12 MINUTES*

(Apply/Review) Distribute a copy of Worksheet 2.4 to each student. If time allows, choose a few students to read the selection aloud in the first part of the worksheet. If not, students should read it independently and answer the follow-up questions in the second part. Correct the answers in class or collect when the lesson is finished.

Optional Bingo Game
10-15 minutes
Photocopy the BINGO cards, markers, and BINGO clues on pages 151-153 and cut out the markers and the individual clues. Distribute one BINGO card and ten markers to each student. Have students put one marker on their free space. Make sure students feel comfortable pronouncing the vocabulary. Put the clues in a container and pick one at random. Read it aloud. Explain to students how to fill out their cards: *The first clue says Clyde B. Wilson. That is a name. Look for one word "name" on your card. Cover it with a marker. The next clue is "February 3, 1999." That is a birth date. Find one phrase "birth date" on your card. Cover it with a marker.* Explain to students that when they cover a line going across, down, or diagonal all the way across the card, they can call out BINGO!

Worksheet 2.4 Note
In this activity, students will encounter unfamiliar words. If their meaning cannot be immediately extrapolated from the text, guide students though a reasoning process that leads to a better understanding of the selection. You can also ask the other students in the class if they have understood the word in question, and encourage those who have to assist their classmates.

Note: To allow for further review, Worksheet 2.5 may be assigned as homework.

Worsheet 2.1: Language Blast

Money

DIRECTIONS Look at the money chart and study the examples.
Then complete the exercises below.

Penny	Nickel	Dime	Quarter	One dollar

1 cent	5 cents	10 cents	25 cents	100 cents

In one dollar there are:
100 pennies (100 x 1 = 100)
20 nickels (20 x 5 = 100)
10 dimes (10 x 10 = 100)
4 quarters (40 x 25 = 100)

In one hundred dollars there are:
100 dollar bills (100 x 1 = 100)
20 five dollar bills (20 x 5 = 100)
10 ten dollar bills (10 x 10 = 100)
2 fifty dollar bills (2 x 50 = 100)

Money Exercises

DIRECTIONS You are earning money. How much money have you earned? Add the
amounts together to get the total.

1.  +   = $1.25

2. + + = _____

3. + + = _____

DIRECTIONS You are spending some of your money. How much do you have left? Subtract
to get the answer.

4.  -   = $5.00

5.  -   = _____

6. -   = _____

Worksheet 2.2: Vocabulary Development

Crossword Puzzle

DIRECTIONS Read the clues. Complete the crossword puzzle with the answers. Use the answer box if you need help.

city	state	birth date	favorite
street	address	phone number	name

Across

1. The number and street where you live is your _____.

5. The thing you like best is your _____.

7. The day on which you were born is your _____.

8. The number (123) 456-7890 is a _____.

Down

As you answer these clues, look at this address:

> Clyde Big
> 54 Easy Avenue
> Chicago, Illinois

2. Illinois is the _____.

3. Easy Avenue is the _____.

4. Chicago is the _____.

6. Clyde Big is the _____.

Worksheet 2.3: Speaking and Listening

Classroom Survey

DIRECTIONS Get to know your classmates. In pairs, ask your partner each question below. Write your partner's name on the line.

Name _____

1. What is your favorite food?

   _____

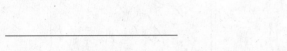

2. What is your favorite book?

   _____

3. What is your favorite movie?

   _____

4. What is your birth date?

   _____

5. What is your phone number?

   _____

Worksheet 2.4: Reading and Fluency

Reading for Understanding

DIRECTIONS Read the story below and use it to help you with the exercise in second part of the worksheet.

DIRECTIONS Answer the following questions in complete sentences.

1. Where does Anita come from? _____

2. Where does Freddy come from? _____

3. What is Anita's phone number? _____

4. What is Anita's address?_____

5. What is Freddy's favorite movie? _____

6. Do Freddy and Anita become friends? _____

7. Who is going to the movie? _____

Worksheet 2.5: Daily Review

Dialogue

DIRECTIONS This boy is looking for a job. He must answer many questions.
Fill in the blanks in this dialogue. Use the boy's answers as clues.

A: What is your _____?

B: I am Joe.

A: What is your _____?

B: I live at 23 Orchard Street.

A: In which _____ and _____

do you live?

B: I live in Hartford, Connecticut.

A: What is your _____?

B: It is (123) 456-7890.

A: What is your _____?

B: I was born on November 1, 1992.

Lesson 3: Daily Routines

STEP 1: WORD DRILL 2 *MINUTES*

(Teach/Guided Practice) Ask the class, *What do you do every day? I brush my hair*. Pantomime brushing your hair. Gesture to the class to repeat: *I brush my hair*. After class has repeated, say: *I brush my hair* again and gesture for the class to repeat. This establishes a rhythm that will always be used to introduce new or difficult words: teacher first and then the class.

(Guided Practice) After class has echoed, point to random individual students, say: *I brush my hair*, and invite the student to repeat alone. Use this routine to introduce new or difficult words to ensure that everybody is pronouncing the words correctly, not only the more outgoing students.

STEP 2: BUILD BACKGROUND 8 *MINUTES*

(Teach/Guided Practice/Practice) Write the short dialogue below on the board. Preteach the necessary vocabulary for the dialogue by using pictures, acting out words, or drawing items on the board. Read the first two lines aloud, and elicit repetition from the students after each line.

Go around the room and let each student have a chance to speak alone. Then continue with the rest of the dialogue. Repeat until students are comfortable pronouncing the words. Say the first line (A), and have the class respond (B). Reverse roles. Divide the class into pairs and assign each partner a role. Allow students to practice the dialogue for one minute while you circulate and monitor progress. Students may vary the dialogue with other activities.

A: What do you do every day?

B: I eat breakfast.

A: What else do you do every day?

B: I go to school. What do you do every day?

A: I go to school, too. After school I play a sport.

B. After school I practice an instrument.

STEP 3: INDEPENDENT RECITATION 3 *MINUTES*

(Apply) If students grasp Step 2 quickly, give them two minutes to memorize the dialogue on the board. When time is up, erase the dialogue and chose a few pairs to recite it from memory for the class.

LESSON OBJECTIVES
Students will:

- respond to basic questions regarding daily routines
- learn nouns used after present tense verbs to describe routine daily activities
- speak in complete, coherent sentences to describe daily routines
- use declarative sentences to describe their own as well as peers' daily routine
- listen to instructions and to their peers' dialogue

LESSON VOCABULARY
Winter, Spring, Summer, Fall, snow, rain, wind, sun, flowers, cold, hot, fallen leaves, get up, go to school, go to sleep, do homework, watch TV, eat lunch, eat dinner, eat breakfast, brush teeth/hair, play a sport, take a shower, practice an instrument

LESSON RESOURCES
Worksheet 3.1
Language Blast: Seasons

Worksheet 3.2
Vocabulary Development: Daily Routine

Worksheet 3.3
Speaking and Listening: Class Survey

Worksheet 3.4
Reading and Fluency

Worksheet 3.5
Daily Review

Teaching Tip Acting out or pantomiming actions is an effective way for students to make a visual and physical connection to the meaning of verbs.

STEP 4: LANGUAGE BLAST *10 MINUTES*

(Teach/Guided Practice/Practice) Tell students there are four seasons in the year, and ask them to name the seasons, if they know them. Write their responses on the board and any seasons that the students did not name. Draw any pictures necessary next to each season to clarify meaning. Point to each season, say it aloud, and have students repeat until they are comfortable pronouncing all four words. Go around the room and call on individual students until each student has said a season. Pass out Worksheet 3.1. Go over the vocabulary and allow students 5-10 minutes to complete the worksheet.

STEP 5: VOCABULARY DEVELOPMENT *10 MINUTES*

(Teach/Practice/Apply) Distribute a copy of Worksheet 3.2 to each student. Begin by asking the students if they recognize any of the vocabulary next to the pictures. Point to each picture and pronounce the words next to it. Invite the class to repeat the vocabulary in unison. Read the paragraph aloud as the students put the pictures in the correct order. Check answers. Then ask students to discuss their daily routines with a partner. Monitor the students' interaction.

STEP 6: GRAMMAR AND CONVENTIONS *15 MINUTES*

(Guided Practice) Ask the class: *Who brushes their teeth every day?* Point to one student who had his/her hand raised. Ask: *Do you brush your teeth every day?* and help the student answer in a complete sentence: *I brush my teeth every day*. Now point to another student and repeat the question. Then point to the first student as you ask the second student: *Does he/she brush his teeth every day?* Help the second student answer: *He/she brushes his teeth every day*. Write *I brush my teeth every day*. and *He/She brushes his/her teeth every day*. on the board, pointing out the difference in the verbs. Underline the subject of each sentence and circle the verbs. Point out the use of *–es* with the subject *he/she* and verb without *–es* with the subject *I*.

SPEAKING AND LISTENING

(Practice/Apply) To reinforce subject/verb agreement and vocabulary comprehension, pass out Worksheet 3.3 and ask the class to complete the worksheet. When they have finished, ask the students to share the information they learned. Then, move on to Worksheet 3.4.

STEP 7: READING AND FLUENCY *12 MINUTES*

(Apply/Review) Distribute a copy of Worksheet 3.4 to each student. If time allows, choose a few students to read the selection aloud. If not, students should read it independently and answer the follow-up questions. Correct the answers in class or collect when the lesson is finished.

Worksheet 3.4 Note
In this activity, students will encounter unfamiliar words. If their meaning cannot be immediately extrapolated from the text, guide students though a reasoning process that leads to a better understanding of the selection. You can also ask the other students in the class if they have understood the word in question, and encourage those who have to assist their classmates.

Note: To allow for further review, Worksheet 3.5 may be assigned as homework.

Worksheet 3.1: Language Blast

Seasons

DIRECTIONS Read the words on the right and match them with the correct season.

snow

rain

wind

sun

flowers

cold

hot

fallen leaves

Worksheet 3.2: Vocabulary Development

Daily Routine

DIRECTIONS As your teacher reads the paragraph aloud, put the images below in the correct order. Number each image from 1–12. Afterwards, discuss with your classmates whether this is a "typical" day or not.

_____ go to school   _____ go to sleep   _____ do homework

_____ get up   _____ watch TV   _____ eat lunch

_____ eat dinner together   _____ at school   _____ go home

_____ eat breakfast   _____ brush teeth   _____ play a sport

Every morning most students get up, they brush their teeth, they take a shower, they eat breakfast, and they go to school. In the afternoon they eat lunch with their friends, they play sports, and then they go home. In the evening, they do their homework, they eat dinner with their family, they watch TV, and they go to sleep.

Is this routine typical of your day?

Worksheet 3.3: Speaking and Listening

Class Survey

DIRECTIONS In small groups ask classmates what they do during the day. Write your classmates' answers in the space provided below. Remember to use correct subject-verb agreement.

Example: What do you do in the morning? I brush my teeth in the morning.

Questions:

What do you do in the morning?

_____

_____

_____

_____

What do you do in the afternoon?

_____

_____

_____

_____

What do you do in the evening?

_____

_____

_____

What do you do at night?

_____

_____

_____

Morning

Afternoon

Evening

Night

Worksheet 3.4: Reading and Fluency

Reading for Understanding

DIRECTIONS Read the story below and use it to help you with the exercise in second part of the worksheet.

DIRECTIONS Read the questions, then use the story to answer each one.

1. What does Tom do every morning at 8?

_____

2. What time does Freddy wake up in the morning?

_____

3. What do Tom and Anita do after school?

_____

4. What does Freddy do while his friends are busy?

_____

5. What do the three friends do together?

_____

Worksheet 3.5: Daily Review

What Do You Do?

DIRECTIONS Fill in the blanks using the correct verb. Be sure that the subject and verb agree.

1. George _____ up every morning at 6.

2. Sally _____ a shower in the morning.

3. Jake says he never _____ his teeth in the morning—gross!

4. I _____ breakfast in the morning.

5. Jerry and Leroy _____ to school on the bus every morning.

6. You _____ lunch every day with your friends.

7. We _____ baseball every afternoon in the spring.

8. Alex _____ football every afternoon in the fall.

9. I _____ home after class.

10. Jane and Steve _____ their instruments in the band every afternoon.

11. Carnie and Terri _____ their homework together in the afternoon.

12. My family _____ dinner together every evening.

13. Jenny _____ TV with her brother sometimes in the evening.

14. My friends and I _____ on the phone sometimes in the evening.

15. Every night I _____.

Lesson 4: Classroom Objects and Supplies
Activities in the Classroom

STEP 1: WORD DRILL *2 MINUTES*
(Teach/Guided Practice) Point to the board and say *board*. Gesture to the class to repeat: *board*. After class has repeated, say: *board* again and gesture for the class to repeat. This establishes a rhythm that is used to introduce new or difficult words: instructor first and then the class.

(Guided Practice) After students have echoed as a class, point to random individual students. Say: *board*, and invite the student to repeat alone. Use this routine to introduce the other new words to ensure that everybody is pronouncing the words correctly, not only by the more outgoing students. Point to or hold up the other classroom objects to teach the vocabulary.

STEP 2: BUILD BACKGROUND *8 MINUTES*
(Teach/Guided Practice/Practice) Write the short dialogue below on the board. Preteach the necessary vocabulary for the dialogue by using pictures, acting out words, or drawing items on the board. Read the first two lines aloud, and elicit repetition from the students after each line.

Go around the room and let each student have a chance to speak alone. Then continue with the rest of the dialogue. Repeat until students are comfortable pronouncing the words. Say the first line (A), and have the class respond (B). Reverse roles. Divide the class into pairs and assign each partner a role. Allow students to practice the dialogue for while you circulate and monitor progress. Students may vary the dialogue with other activities.

A: Excuse me, can you tell me what the homework is?

B: We need to read a chapter in the textbook.

A: Thank you.

B: You are welcome. Do you have a pencil I can use?

A: Yes, I have a pencil you can use.

B: Thank you.

STEP 3: INDEPENDENT RECITATION *3 MINUTES*
(Apply) If students grasp Step 2 quickly, give them two minutes to memorize the dialogue on the board. When time is up, erase the dialogue and chose a few pairs to recite it from memory in front of the class.

LESSON OBJECTIVES
Students will:
- respond to basic questions regarding classroom objects and activities
- learn nouns used after present tense verbs to describe classroom objects and activities
- speak in complete, coherent sentences to describe classroom objects and activities
- use interrogative sentences to ask peers about classroom objects and activities
- listen to instructions and to their peers' dialogue

LESSON VOCABULARY
desk, board, clock, computer, map, chair, ruler, eraser, pencil, paper, textbook, notebook (and pass tests, ask questions, finish homework, solve problems, take notes, teach lessons, help classmates)

LESSON RESOURCES
Worksheet 4.1
Language Blast:
Days of the Week

Worksheet 4.2
Vocabulary Development:
Classroom Objects and
Supplies

Worksheet 4.3
Speaking and Listening:
Matching and Speaking

Worksheet 4.4
Reading and Fluency

Worksheet 4.5
Daily Review

STEP 4: LANGUAGE BLAST *10 MINUTES*

(Teach/Guided Practice/Practice) Ask students to name the days of the week, if they know them. Write the days of the week on the board. Circle today's day. Say: *Today is (day)*. Point to each day, say it aloud, and have students repeat until they are comfortable pronouncing the days. Call out a day. Call on individual students to say the day of the week that follows. Continue until each student has said a day. Point out that Saturday and Sunday are the *weekend*. Pass out Worksheet 4.1 and allow students 5–10 minutes to complete it. Do an example with the class.

STEP 5: VOCABULARY DEVELOPMENT *10 MINUTES*

(Teach/Practice/Apply) Distribute a copy of Worksheet 4.2 to each student. Begin by asking the students if they recognize any of the vocabulary next to the pictures. Have students share words they know. Point to each picture and pronounce the word next to it. Invite the class to repeat the vocabulary in unison. Have students point out any of the items that are in the classroom and identify them. Then ask students to complete the worksheet in pairs. Monitor the students' interaction and correct pronunciation as necessary.

STEP 6: GRAMMAR AND CONVENTIONS *15 MINUTES*

(Guided Practice) Ask the class: *What do we do at school?* Help them answer: *We ask questions*. Repeat several times, and then ask students to say it with you: *We ask questions*. Act out, draw, or explain as necessary.

Go around the room and call on individual students. Ask: *What do we do at school?* Help the student answer: *We pass tests*. Vary the answer to include all of the classroom activities vocabulary. Act out, draw, or explain the meaning of the vocabulary as necessary. Write *What do we do at school?* on the board, and underline the question mark. Tell students that interrogative sentences ask questions. When they are reading, they can recognize interrogative sentences by the question mark at the end. When they are speaking, they can recognize interrogative sentences by the speaker's voice. Model for students the way that a speaker raises their voice slightly at the end of a question, and have students repeat after you. Point out the use of *do* in the question. Tell students that we use the auxiliary verb *do* or *does* in questions about the present for regular verbs. Model examples for the students to illustrate the use of *do* and *does* in questions.

Teaching Tip Asking yes/no and embedded questions is a good way to check your students' comprehension. To check vocabulary comprehension, hold up a pencil and ask: *Is this a book?* or *Is this a pencil or a book?*

Note: To allow for further review, Worksheet 4.5 may be assigned as homework.

SPEAKING AND LISTENING

(Practice/Apply) To reinforce interrogative sentences, as well as vocabulary comprehension, distribute Worksheet 4.3 and ask the class to work in pairs to match the pictures with the questions (35 min). After the activity has been completed, cue the one student in to choose a question from the worksheet to ask a classmate. Have the second student answer the question in a complete sentence. After the response, have the class say what the student does, using the third person. Then ask the student who answered to take a turn asking somebody else a question. Model an example with the students, both for affirmative and negative responses. Afterwards move on to Worksheet 4.4.

STEP 7: READING AND FLUENCY *12 MINUTES*

(Apply/Review) Distribute a copy of Worksheet 4.4 to each student. If time allows, choose a few students to read aloud the selection in the first part of the worksheet. If not, students should read it independently and answer the follow-up questions in the second part. Correct in class or collect when the lesson is finished.

Worksheet 4.4 Note
In this activity, students will encounter unfamiliar words. If their meaning cannot be immediately extrapolated from the text, guide students though a reasoning process that leads to a better understanding of the selection. You can also ask the other students in the class if they have understood the word in question, and encourage those who have to assist their classmates.

Worksheet 4.1: Language Blast

Days of the Week

DIRECTIONS Listen as your teacher reads the days of the week below. Repeat the days of the week aloud with your classmates, and then answer the following questions by yourself.

Sunday (Weekend!)	Monday (School)	Tuesday (School)	Wednesday (School)	Thursday (School)	Friday (School)	Saturday (Weekend!)

1. I go to school on (five days): _____.

2. I stay home on (two days): _____.

3. The first day of school every week is _____.

4. The last day of school every week is _____.

5. The 1st day is Sunday. The 3rd day is _____.

6. The 3rd day is Tuesday. The 7th day is _____.

7. The 7th day is Saturday. The 8th day is _____.

8. The 2nd day is Monday. The 6th day is _____.

9. The 5th day is Thursday. The 7th day is _____.

10. My favorite day of the week is _____ because _____.

Worksheet 4.2: Vocabulary Development

Classroom Objects and Supplies

DIRECTIONS Review the following vocabulary words together with your teacher. Then unscramble the words below and match them to the pictures.

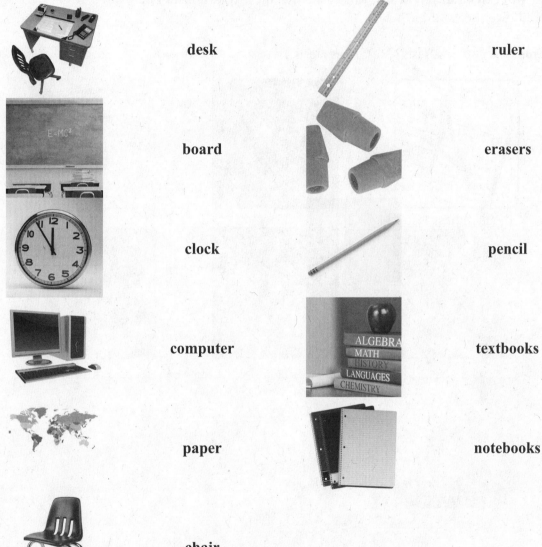

desk		ruler
board		erasers
clock		pencil
computer		textbooks
paper		notebooks
chair		

bntosekoo _____   lcipne _____   lrure _____

kdse _____   appre _____   kxtosetob _____

murtocpe _____   robad, _____   colck _____

icrah _____   serares _____

Worksheet 4.3: Speaking and Listening

Matching

DIRECTIONS Look at the pictures and read the questions. Write the question that matches the picture on the line below each picture. Afterwards your teacher will call on different students to answer these questions, so be prepared! See the example below.

Example: Do you pass tests? Yes, I pass tests.

1. <u>Yes, I pass tests.</u>

2. _____

3. _____

4. _____

5. _____

6. _____

7. _____

Do you teach lessons?

Do you finish your homework?

Do you pass tests?

Do you solve problems?

Do you help your classmates?

Do you take notes?

Do you ask questions?

Worksheet 4.4: Reading and Fluency

Reading for Understanding

DIRECTIONS Read the comic strip below and label the sentences *True* or
False. Rewrite false sentences to make them true in the space provided.

1. Anita, Tom, and Freddy do not pass tests.

_____

2. Tom and Freddy like school.

_____

3. Tom and Freddy do not need to pass tests to play soccer and practice the saxophone.

_____

4. Anita offers to help Tom and Freddy.

_____

5. Tom and Freddy do not pass tests, even with Anita's help.

_____

Worksheet 4.5: Daily Review

Who Asks Each Question?

DIRECTIONS Read the following questions and identify who asks you these questions using the three choices below. More than one person may ask some of the questions.

A. Teacher   **B. Parents**   **C. Coach**

1. Do you pass tests?

_____

2. Do you finish your homework?

_____

3. Do you ask questions?

_____

4. Do you help others?

_____

5. Do you practice an instrument?

_____

6. Do you practice a sport?

_____

7. Do you solve problems?

_____

8. Do you go to work?

_____

Lesson 5: In Case of Emergency

STEP 1: WORD DRILL *2 MINUTES*

(Teach/Guided Practice) Greet the class and say that you are going to play a game called "Emergency." Say: *I'll tell you the emergency and you say, 'Call for help!'* Model saying: *Call for help!* enthusiastically and have students echo. Now establish a rhythm in which you say: *Emergency!* and students reply: *Call for help!*

(Guided Practice) After students have established this pattern, replace *Emergency* with the following: *Earthquake!, Fire!, Flood!*, while students reply to each with: *Call for help!* Draw pictures of each emergency situation as you call out the word. Help students as needed to ensure that they are pronouncing words correctly.

STEP 2: BUILD BACKGROUND *8 MINUTES*

(Teach/Guided Practice/Practice) Write the three short dialogues below on the board. Preteach or review the vocabulary necessary for the dialogues. Read the first pair of lines aloud and then point to random students, asking them to say these lines out loud. Repeat this exercise for all three pairs of lines. Help students with proper pronunciation. Point to the words on the board as you read.

Now, erase the word, *firefighters*, from the first dialogue. Choose several students to read aloud the first dialogue, filling in the blank with the proper word. Repeat with the second dialogue, erasing the word, *police*, and then the third dialogue, erasing the word *paramedics*. Allow each student to try this exercise, offering help as needed.

A: Help! Fire! Call the firefighters!

B: I will call 911!

A: Help! Robbers! Get the police!

B: I'll call 911!

A: Help! I hurt myself! Call the paramedics!

B: I'll call 911!

STEP 3: INDEPENDENT RECITATION *3 MINUTES*

(Apply) If students grasp Step 2 quickly, give them 1 minute to memorize each of the three pairs of lines on the board. When time is up, erase that pair of lines and chose a few students to recite them from memory in front of the class.

LESSON OBJECTIVES
Students will:
- recognize and correctly pronounce words when reading aloud
- produce vocabulary to communicate emergency needs
- demonstrate comprehension of vocabulary by using 1-2 words or a simple sentence response
- learn how to construct simple imperative sentences
- use imperative sentences correctly in speaking
- listen to instructions and to their peers' dialogue

LESSON VOCABULARY
Go to the doctor, call the police, call for help, police officer, paramedic, firefighter, nurse, hospital, police station, bandage, earthquake, fire, flood

LESSON RESOURCES
Worksheet 5.1
Language Blast:
Daily Routine

Worksheet 5.2
Vocabulary Development:
Vocabulary Match

Worksheet 5.3
Speaking and Listening:
Emergency Plans

Worksheet 5.4
Reading and Fluency

Worksheet 5.5
Daily Review

STEP 4: LANGUAGE BLAST *10 MINUTES*

(Teach/Guided Practice/Practice) Write the Daily Routine vocabulary words on the board. Review words with students, asking them to echo read each phrase. Call on students to pantomime the actions depicted by each phrase to show comprehension. Pass out Worksheet 5.1 and read the directions aloud. Allow students 510 minutes to complete the worksheet. When they are done, review the order of the daily routine on the worksheet and write the answers on the board in a column. Have the students transform each activity into a sentence starting with *I*. Next, ask students to turn over their worksheets so they cannot see their answers. Go around the room and ask individual students to each read one line from the column on the board. Then erase a random line on the board. Go around the room again asking students to each read a line. When a student reaches the missing line, have him or her fill in the missing activity. Erase lines one at a time until the class can independently recite the daily routine.

STEP 5: VOCABULARY DEVELOPMENT *10 MINUTES*

(Teach/Practice/Apply) Distribute a copy of Worksheet 5.2 to each student. Read the directions aloud on the top of the page and allow students 34 minutes to match the captions with the pictures. When they have finished, go over the vocabulary with students, reading each vocabulary item aloud. Ask students to repeat the words. Next, read the directions aloud on the second half of the page. Have students sort the vocabulary items into nouns or verbs. Review nouns and verbs as necessary. Allow students 34 minutes to complete the exercise and circulate around the room monitoring progress. Check answers as a class when students have completed the exercises.

STEP 6: GRAMMAR AND CONVENTIONS *15 MINUTES*

(Guided Practice) Tell students that imperative sentences are commands that tell people what to do. Imperative sentences start with a verb, or an action word, such as *Go* away or *Call* the doctor. Tell students they will make an imperative sentence for different kinds of emergencies. Say: *I broke my arm.* Act out breaking your arm. Then tell the class: *Now you say 'Call the doctor.'* Ask class to repeat the command. Write the sentence on the board. Circle the verb. Next, say: *There's a fire.* Students should say: *Call the firefighters.* Prompt class as needed by saying, *Call the ____.* Continue by saying: *There's a robber* with students responding: *Call the police.* Ask several students to try leading the class, thinking of different kinds of emergencies.

Teaching Tip Make pronunciation easier for students by breaking up longer words into syllables. To help students isolate sounds, start their pronunciation with the last syllable, gradually adding the other syllables until they can say the whole word.

Note: To allow for further review, Worksheet 5.5 may be assigned as homework.

SPEAKING AND LISTENING

(Practice/Apply) Divide students into groups of 3 or 4 and distribute Worksheet 5.3. Go over each emergency situation and possible plans of action with students. Preteach or review any vocabulary, as necessary. Give students 5 minutes to discuss each situation within their groups, choosing an appropriate plan of action from the list. Monitor while students speak about what they would do in each situation. Then, for each situation, ask groups to share their plans of action with the class. If there is time, have them act out the situations and plans of action.

STEP 7: READING AND FLUENCY *12 MINUTES*

(Apply/Review) Distribute a copy of Worksheet 5.4 to each student. If time allows, choose a few students to read aloud the selection in the first part of the worksheet. If not, students should read it independently and answer the follow-up questions. Correct in class or collect when lesson is finished.

Distribute Worksheet 5.5, Imperative Commands. Read the directions aloud and preteach any new vocabulary. Complete example with the class and then allow students to complete the rest of the matching exercise. When complete, review the completed commands. Ask students to repeat each of them in unison.

Worksheet 5.1: Language Blast

Daily Routine

DIRECTIONS Look at the pictures. Write the correct activity on the line under each picture.

_____

_____

_____

_____

_____

_____

_____

_____

_____

_____

_____

_____

Worksheet 5.2: Vocabulary Development

Vocabulary Match

DIRECTIONS Look at the following pictures. Choose the correct vocabulary word or phrase from the word bank and write it under each picture.

1. _____

2. _____

3. _____

4. _____

5. _____

6. _____

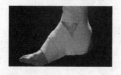

7. _____

8. _____

9. _____

Word Bank

police officer	fire	hospital	earthquake	bandage
firefighter	call for help	nurse	go to the doctor	

DIRECTIONS Look at the words under each picture. Which words are nouns? Which words are verbs? Write the nouns in one column. Write the verbs in the other column.

Verbs	Nouns

Worksheet 5.3: Speaking and Listening

Emergency Plans

DIRECTIONS In a small group, talk about the most important thing to do during each emergency. Choose from the plans of action listed below and draw lines matching each emergency to a plan of action. More than one plan of action can match each emergency.

Emergencies	Plans of Action
1. Fire	1. Call 911 for the police.
2. Flood	2. Call 911 for the paramedics.
3. Earthquake	3. Call 911 for the firefighters.
4. Robbery	4. Evacuate the building.
5. Bleeding arm	5. Use a bandage.
6. Car accident	6. Go to the hospital.
	7. Get under your desk.
	8. Put pressure on the wound
	9. Unplug electrical things.

Worksheet 5.4: Reading and Fluency

Reading for Understanding

DIRECTIONS Read the following dialogue.

DIRECTIONS Answer the questions below and circle the correct answers.

1. What did Tom, Freddy, and Anita see at the school?

    A. a robber

    B. a fire

2. Who said "Quick, call for help!"

    A. Freddy

    B. Tom

3. What did Anita do?

    A. call the school

    B. call 9-1-1

4. What did Anita say on the phone?

    A. There is a fire – come quickly!

    B. I am at school.

Worksheet 5.5: Daily Review

Imperative Commands

DIRECTIONS Match each verb with a word or phrase to make a command.
Write the letter of the correct phrase next to each verb. Then say each
phrase aloud.

Verbs

_____ 1. Go ____ _____

_____ 2. Go _____

_____ 3. Study___ ____ _____

_____ 4. Eat ____ _____

_____ 5. Be _____

_____ 6. Be _____

_____ 7. Pay _____

_____ 8. Listen _____

_____ 9. Call ____ _____

Phrases

a. nice

b. your dinner

c. quiet

d. attention

e. for your exam

f. away

g. the police

h. closely

i. to sleep

Lesson 6: Activities with Friends

STEP 1: WORD DRILL *2 MINUTES*

(Teach/Guided Practice) Greet the class and say: *There are so many things I like to do! I like reading a _____.* Instead of saying *book*, mime reading a book and let students guess the word. Praise them and complete the phrase, saying: *reading a book.* Ask students to repeat the phrase chorally.

(Guided Practice) When students understand the pattern, say: *I also like talking on the ___.* Mime talking on the phone. After students guess correctly, say the phrase: *talking on the phone,* and have them repeat it chorally. Continue the same pattern with the phrases, *singing a <u>song</u>,* and *listening to <u>music</u>.* Help students as needed to ensure that they are pronouncing the vocabulary correctly.

STEP 2: BUILD BACKGROUND *8 MINUTES*

(Teach/Guided Practice/Practice) This is a continuation of Step 1 and can be used to help students become more familiar with the vocabulary and the concept of "activities." Write the short dialogue below on the board. Say: *There are so many things I like to do. I like listening to music and reading a book. I like going out and eating a meal. I like watching a movie, and talking on the phone. These things are called activities. Activities are things to do.* Ask students to say the word *activities.*

Read the first two lines aloud. Then point to individual students, asking the question in line A and eliciting a correct response for line B. Repeat this exercise with different students for all three pairs of lines. Next, have partners practice asking and answering the dialogue questions. Circulate around the room and monitor pronunciation as students practice.

A: What is your favorite activity?

B: My favorite activity is _____.

A: What is your least favorite activity?

B: My least favorite activity is _____.

A: What after-school activity do you like?

B: An after-school activity I like is _____.

LESSON OBJECTIVES
Students will:

- recognize and correctly pronounce vocabulary words when reading aloud
- respond to questions with appropriate short phrases
- recognize present progressive verb forms
- learn how to create sentences with present progressive verb forms
- use vocabulary correctly in simple sentences during interactions with peers
- understand and follow simple multiple-step oral directions.

LESSON VOCABULARY
January, February, March, April, May, June, July, August, September, October, November, December, playing a game, reading a book, listening to music, singing a song, eating a meal, walking to school, going out, watching a movie, talking on the phone

LESSON RESOURCES
Worksheet 6.1
Language Blast: Months of the Year

Worksheet 6.2
Vocabulary Development: Matching

Worksheet 6.3
Speaking and Listening: What Do You Like To Do?

Worksheet 6.4
Reading and Fluency

Worksheet 6.5
Daily Review

STEP 3: INDEPENDENT RECITATION *3 MINUTES*

(Apply) If students grasp Step 2 quickly, give them 1 minute to memorize each of the three line pairs on the board. When time is up, erase the lines and chose a few students to recite each pair in front of the class.

STEP 4: LANGUAGE BLAST *10 MINUTES*

(Teach/Guided Practice/Practice) Show students a calendar. Ask them if they know what month it is now. Distribute Worksheet 6.1 and review the months of the year with students, having them echo each month out loud. Make sure students correctly pronounce each word. Next, read the directions to Part B and complete the first question together. Read the remainder of the questions together with students, going over any unfamiliar words. Allow students approximately 10 minutes to complete the worksheet independently, offering assistance as needed.

STEP 5: VOCABULARY DEVELOPMENT *10 MINUTES*

(Teach/Practice/Apply) Distribute a copy of Worksheet 6.2 to each student and quickly review the pictures and captions. Have students work with partners to match captions and pictures. When they are done, review the answers, correcting them as necessary. Next, read aloud the directions for part C. Remind students of the dialogue in Step 2, which focused on favorite and least-favorite activities. Ask students to think of each activity, asking themselves which they like best, next best, and so on, until all of the activities are rated. Ask volunteers to share their responses.

STEP 6: GRAMMAR AND CONVENTIONS *15 MINUTES*

(Guided Practice) Write on the board, *I like _____.* Say to the class: *I like _____* as you mime reading. Have students supply the word *reading*. Write it in the blank on the board. Now say: *I like _____.* and mime singing. When students guess correctly, write *I am singing* on the board. In the two sentences, underline the word *like* and the *ing*. Point out to students that the second verb in these sentences has *ing* added. Have students help you complete these examples on the board: *I read. I like reading. He walks. He likes walking. They eat. They like eating.*

Teaching Tip To reinforce the present progressive, point out examples of present progressive as you teach throughout the day, writing the sentences on the board and underlining the *ing*.

Note: To allow for further review, Worksheet 6.5 may be assigned as homework.

SPEAKING AND LISTENING

(Practice/Apply) Distribute Worksheet 6.3. Have students underline the instances of *ing* in the vocabulary box. Then have students complete the worksheet. As students read the dialogue in pairs, circulate and give feedback about correct pronunciation.

STEP 7: READING AND FLUENCY *12 MINUTES*

(Apply/Review) Distribute Worksheet 6.4. Go over the directions and select a few students to read the comic aloud. Ask the class to complete the questions independently. Correct the Worksheet together and move on to Worksheet 6.5.

Worksheet 6.1: Language Blast

Months of the Year

DIRECTIONS Review the vocabulary below with your teacher.

January	April	July	October
February	May	August	November
March	June	September	December

DIRECTIONS Fill in the sentences using the vocabulary above.

1. Christmas is in _____.

2. Summer vacation begins in _____.

3. My birthday is in _____.

4. School begins in _____.

5. School ends in _____.

6. Halloween is in _____.

7. Thanksgiving is in _____.

8. New Year's Day is in _____.

9. Independence Day is in _____.

10. My best friend's birthday is in _____.

11. My mother's birthday is in_____.

12. My father's birthday is in _____.

13. My favorite month of the year is _____.

14. My least favorite month of the year is _____.

Worksheet 6.2: Vocabulary Development

Matching

DIRECTIONS Look at the pictures in Part A. Read the captions in Part B.
Write the letter of the matching caption on the line under each picture.

PART A

1._____

2._____

3._____

4._____

5._____

6._____

7._____

8._____

9._____

PART B

A. Singing a song

B. Eating a meal

C. Listening to music

D. Watching a movie

E. Going out with friends

F. Playing a game

G. Walking to school

H. Talking on the phone

I. Reading a book

PART C

DIRECTIONS Rate each of the activities from your least favorite to your most
favorite. Use 1 for your most favorite activity and 9 for your least favorite.
Write the number on the line under each picture.

Worksheet 6.3: Speaking and Listening

What Do You Like To Do?

DIRECTIONS Read this dialogue with a partner. Fill in the blanks using vocabulary from the box below. When you are done, check each other's answers and read the dialogue together.

singing	listening	eating
watching	going	playing
walking	talking	reading

Student A: I do not know you very well.
What do you like to do?

Student B: I like _____ to music.
What is your favorite thing to do?

Student A: My favorite thing is _____ on the phone.
I do that while I am _____ to school.

Student B: I like _____ a nice dinner.
Then I like _____ a movie or _____ a game.

Student A: I like to do those things, too. I also like _____ a book.
Sometimes my friends and I try _____ a song.

Student B: I like singing, too. I also like _____ out with friends.
Now you are a friend. Maybe you can go out with us, too.

Worksheet 6.4: Reading and Fluency

Reading for Understanding

DIRECTIONS   Read the following dialogue.

DIRECTIONS Circle the sentences that are true. Rewrite sentences that are false.

1. James is watching a movie. _____.

2. Yolanda listens to the music, too. _____.

3. Yolanda plays the clarinet. _____.

4. James plays the drums. _____.

5. Yolanda and James decide to start a band. _____.

6. Yolanda has to be in class in 10 minutes? _____.

7. Yolanda and James will meet after work. _____.

8. They need to find a drummer and a singer for their band. _____.

Worksheet 6.5: Daily Review

What Are They Doing?

DIRECTIONS Look at the pictures. Each picture should have a question and an answer underneath it. Fill in the blanks under each picture with the missing question or answer. The first one is done for you.

1. <u>What are they doing?</u>
They are playing a game.

2. _____
She is reading a book.

3. _____
They are watching a movie.

4. _____
He is listening to music.

5. _____ <u>What is she doing?</u>

6. _____
They are eating a meal.

7. What are the students doing?

8. _____
The friends are going out.

9. <u>What is the man doing?</u>

Lesson 7: What Are You Doing?

STEP 1: WORD DRILL *2 MINUTES*
(Teach/Guided Practice) Pantomime holding a phone in your hand and dialing a number. Hold the phone close to your ear. Say: *Hello, Jane. What are you doing?* Gesture to the class to repeat. After repetition, say the question again and cue the class to repeat. This establishes a rhythm that will be used to introduce new or difficult words: teacher first and then the class.

(Guided Practice) After class has echoed, point to individuals and say: *Hello, Jane. What are you doing?* Cue the student to repeat the dialogue. Use this routine when introducing new words so that the words are being pronounced correctly by everybody, not only by the more outgoing students.

STEP 2: BUILD BACKGROUND *8 MINUTES*
(Teach/Guided Practice/Practice) Write the short dialogue below on the board. Preteach the necessary vocabulary by using pictures, acting out words, or drawing items on the board. Read the first two lines aloud, and elicit repetition from the students after each line.

Let each student have a chance to speak alone. Then continue with the dialogue. Repeat until students are comfortable pronouncing the words. Divide the class into pairs and assign each partner a role. Allow students to practice the dialogue for one minute while you circulate and monitor progress. Students may vary the dialogue with other activities.

A: Hello, _____. How are you?

B: I'm fine, thank you.

A: What are you doing?

B: I am reading a book. What are you doing?

A: I am going to the park.

B. I will see you there when I finish reading.

STEP 3: INDEPENDENT RECITATION *3 MINUTES*
(Apply) If students quickly grasp Step 2, give them two minutes to memorize the dialogue on the board. When time is up, erase the dialogue and chose a few pairs to recite it from memory to the class.

STEP 4: LANGUAGE BLAST *10 MINUTES*
(Teach/Guided Practice/Practice) Ask students to name today's day of the week. Write it on the board. Ask students to name the other days of the week. Write them on the board. Repeat this routine with the months. Point to each day and month, say it aloud, and have students repeat until they are comfortable pronouncing all nineteen words.

LESSON OBJECTIVES
Students will:
- respond to basic questions regarding daily activities in the context of a telephone conversation
- learn nouns used after present tense verbs to communicate daily activities in social situations
- speak in complete, coherent sentences to communicate daily activities in social situations
- use interrogative sentences in social situations, such as a telephone conversation
- listen to instructions and to their peers' dialogue

LESSON VOCABULARY
playing a game, reading a book, listening to music, singing a song, eating a meal, walking to school, going out, watching a movie, talking on the phone, Who? What? When? Where? Why? How?

LESSON RESOURCES
Worksheet 7.1
Language Blast: Review Days of the Week and Months of the Year

Worksheet 7.2
Vocabulary Development: Matching and Speaking

Worksheet 7.3
Speaking and Listening: What Are the Students Doing?

Worksheet 7.4
Reading and Fluency

Worksheet 7.5
Daily Review

Call out a day. Then go around the room and cue individual students to say the day of the week that follows. Continue until each student has said a day. Repeat this with the months. Pass out Worksheet 7.1 and allow students 510 minutes to complete it. Make sure students know the meaning of *before* and *after*.

STEP 5: VOCABULARY DEVELOPMENT *10 MINUTES*

(Teach/Practice/Apply) Write the question words that appear on Worksheet 7.2 on the board. Ask the students if they know any of the words. Have students share any words that they know. Explain the meaning of any unfamiliar words. Point to and say each word. Have students repeat the words after you. Explain that we can change the meaning of a question by changing the interrogative word. Model an example for the students. Distribute a copy of Worksheet 7.2 to each student. Have the students use the words to complete the sentences. Check answers. Review the interrogative structure with the students. Then ask students to complete the second part of the worksheet in pairs. Monitor the students' interaction and correct as necessary.

STEP 6: GRAMMAR AND CONVENTIONS *15 MINUTES*

(Guided Practice) Ask the class: *What are you doing?* Pantomime reading and say: *I am reading.* After repeating several times, ask students to say it with you: *I am reading.*

Ask individual students: *What are you doing?* Help the student answer: *I am reading.* Write the sentence on the board. Underline *am* in the sentence and circle the *-ing* in the verb. Explain that we use the verb *be* with the verb with *-ing* to talk about what someone is doing at the moment. Pantomime different activities to include all of the classroom vocabulary activities and prompt students to say what you are doing. Have student volunteers pantomime different actions. Point to individuals and ask the class: *What is (student) doing?*

SPEAKING AND LISTENING

(Practice/Apply) To reinforce interrogative sentences and the present progressive, distribute Worksheet 7.3. Ask the class to match the pictures to the activities. Then have the students work in pairs to answer questions about the pictures.

STEP 7: READING AND FLUENCY *12 MINUTES*

(Apply/Review) Distribute a copy of Worksheet 7.4 to each student. If time allows, choose a few students to read the first part of the worksheet aloud. If not, students should read it independently and answer the follow-up questions in the second part. Correct in class or collect when the lesson is finished.

Teaching Tip Randomly calling on students can be a good way to keep the class alert and active in an activity.

Optional Game: Charades
10-15 minutes
Photocopy Charades game on page 154. The phrases on the page should be photocopied, cut into strips, and placed into a bag or a cup. Make sure students feel comfortable pronouncing the vocabulary before starting. Choose a student volunteer to pick out one of the phrases from the bag to act out. Ask the class: *What is (student) doing*? Have the class guess what the student is doing. Encourage them to use complete sentences. To vary the verb forms, have two or three students act out the same phrase to practice the plural forms.

Worksheet 7.4 Note
In this activity, students will encounter unfamiliar words. If their meaning cannot be immediately extrapolated from the text, guide students though a reasoning process that leads to a better understanding of the selection. You can also ask the other students in the class if they have understood the word in question, and encourage those who have to assist their classmates.

Note: To allow for further review, Worksheet 7.5 may be assigned as homework

Worksheet 7.1: Language Blast

Months of the Year/Days of the Week

DIRECTIONS Using words below, complete the following crossword puzzle.
The first one has been done for you.

ACROSS:

3. The first month of the year.

5. The day after Saturday.

7. The month after July.

8. The day before Thursday.

12. The last month of the year.

DOWN:

1. The day before Friday.

2. The month after February.

4. The month before July.

6. The month after August.

9. The month before November.

10. The day before Tuesday.

11. The month before May.

January	October	April	Wednesday	August	Sunday
June	Thursday	March	Monday	December	September

Worksheet 7.2: Vocabulary Development

Matching and Speaking

DIRECTIONS Use the question words in the word bank to complete the
sentences below.

Word Bank

what	how	where	when	why	who

1. _____ time is it?

2. _____ do you go after school?

3. _____ is the sky blue?

4. _____ do you want to learn English?

5. _____ is your friend?

6. _____ is your name?

7. _____ do you live?

8. _____ do you say that in English?

9. _____ is that girl?

10. _____ does the movie start?

DIRECTIONS Work with your partner to create three more questions using
the word bank. Be ready to share them with the class when your teacher calls
on you.

11. _____

12. _____

13. _____

Worksheet 7.3: Speaking and Listening

What Are the Students Doing?

DIRECTIONS Match the activities to the pictures. After you finish, take turns asking and answering questions about the pictures with your partner. Follow the example.

Example: What are the students doing? The students are playing a game.

1. _____

2. _____

3. _____

4. _____

5. _____

6. _____

7. _____

8. _____

9. _____

going out
playing a game
talking on the phone

watching a movie
listening to music
eating a meal

reading a book
singing a song
walking to school

Worksheet 7.4: Reading and Fluency

Reading for Understanding

DIRECTIONS After you read the comic strip, read the questions below.
Circle each correct sentence.

1. What are Alex, James, and Yolanda doing?

   A. Alex, James, and Yolanda are talking.

   B. Alex, James, and Yolanda are working on their homework.

2. Where are Alex, James, and Yolanda?

   A. Alex, James, and Yolanda are in the café.

   B. Alex, James, and Yolanda are at school.

3. Who does Alex know?

   A. Alex knows a singer.

   B. Alex knows a drummer.

4. What is Alex's friend doing?

   A. He is watching a movie.

   B. He is studying in a café.

Worksheet 7.5: Daily Review

What Are They Doing?

DIRECTIONS Complete the dialog by filling in the blanks with a word from the word bank below. Some words may be used more than once. When you have finished, read the dialogue aloud with a partner.

A. Hello, what _____ you _____?

B. I _____ _____ a book. What _____ you _____

A. I _____ _____ a movie. What _____ the others _____?

B. Sue _____ _____ to music.

A. Is Ramon _____ to music, too?

B. No. Ramon _____ _____ a song.

A. Is Kate _____ a song?

B. No. Kate _____ _____ on the phone.

A. I _____ _____ out. Goodbye.

B. Goodbye.

Word Bank

am	is	are	doing	reading
singing	watching	going	going	

Lesson 8: Types of Classes

STEP 1: WORD DRILL *2 MINUTES*
(Teach/Guided Practice) Say to students: *Our class is Language Arts*. Gesture to the class to repeat: *Our class is Language Arts*. After class has repeated, say the sentence again and gesture for the class to repeat.

(Guided Practice) After students have echoed as a class, point to random individual students. Say: *Our class is Language Arts*, and invite the student to repeat alone. Use this routine when introducing new words to ensure that the words are being pronounced correctly by everybody, not only by the more outgoing students.

STEP 2: BUILD BACKGROUND *8 MINUTES*
(Teach/Guided Practice/Practice) Write the short dialogue below on the board. Preteach the necessary vocabulary for the dialogue by using pictures, acting out words, or drawing items on the board. Read the first two lines aloud, and elicit repetition from the students after each line.

Go around the room and let each student have a chance to speak alone. Then continue with the rest of the dialogue. Repeat until students are comfortable pronouncing the words. Say the first line (A), and have the class respond (B). Reverse roles. When results are satisfactory. Divide the class into pairs and assign each partner a role. Allow students to practice the dialogue for while you circulate and monitor progress. Students may vary the dialogue with other subjects.

A: Which class do you have before lunch?

B: I have Math class before lunch.

A: I have Science class before lunch. Which class does Amy have?

B: She has Chemistry class before lunch.

A: I think Amy has Math class before lunch.

B. No, she has Chemistry class before lunch.

STEP 3: INDEPENDENT RECITATION *3 MINUTES*
(Apply) If students quickly grasp Step 2 quickly, give them two minutes to memorize the dialogue on the board. When time is up, erase the dialogue and chose a few pairs to recite it from memory for the class.

STEP 4: LANGUAGE BLAST *10 MINUTES*
(Teach/Guided Practice/Practice) Point to your head and say: *head*. Gesture for students to repeat: *head*. Continue this routine until all vocabulary words have been used and students are comfortable pronouncing the words. Then go around the room and call on individual students, pointing to different body parts, until each student has named at least one body part. Pass out Worksheet 8.1 and allow students 510 minutes to complete it.

LESSON OBJECTIVES
Students will:

- respond to basic questions regarding different types of classes at school
- learn possessive nouns and adjectives used to describe different parts of the body
- speak in simple sentences to communicate different types of classes at school
- use interrogative sentences to ask peers about different types of classes at school
- listen to instructions and to their peers' dialogue

LESSON VOCABULARY
Language Arts, Math, Physical Education (Phys Ed), Social Studies, Homeroom, Chemistry, Art, Music, Science, Biology, History, hair, head, shoulders, neck, throat, back, chest, stomach, arms, elbows, hands, wrists, fingers, legs, knees, ankles, feet, toes, face, ears, nose, eyes, mouth, tongue, cheeks, eyebrows, teeth, lips

LESSON RESOURCES
Worksheet 8.1
Language Blast:
Parts of the Body

Worksheet 8.2
Vocabulary Development:
Image & Word Match

Worksheet 8.3
Speaking and Listening:
Class Interviews

Worksheet 8.4
Reading and Fluency

Worksheet 8.5
Daily Review

STEP 5: VOCABULARY DEVELOPMENT *10 MINUTES*

(Teach/Practice/Apply) Distribute a copy of Worksheet 8.2 to each student. Begin by asking the students if they recognize any of the vocabulary words next to the pictures. Have them share any words that they know. Point to each picture and pronounce the word next to it. Invite the class to repeat the vocabulary in unison. Then ask students to complete the exercise in pairs. Monitor the students' interaction and correct pronunciation as needed.

STEP 6: GRAMMAR AND CONVENTIONS *15 MINUTES*

(Guided Practice) Ask students: *Which class is Roger taking?* Model the answer: *Roger's class is Science.* Write *Roger's class is Science.* on the board, and underline the possessive noun. Tell students that the apostrophe and the letter *s* indicate possession. Repeat the sentence and then ask students to say it with you: *Roger's class is Science.*

Go around the room and call on individual students. Ask: *Which class is Roger taking?* Help the student answer: *Roger's class is Science.* Write the different class names on the board. Point to different classes as you ask the question to prompt student responses. Vary the names and the classes as you call on different students. Use the same routine to teach the possessive adjectives.

SPEAKING AND LISTENING

(Practice/Apply) To reinforce possessive nouns and adjectives, as well as vocabulary comprehension, pass out Worksheet 8.3 and ask the class to complete it. Review their findings and move on to Worksheet 8.4.

STEP 7: READING AND FLUENCY *12 MINUTES*

(Apply/Review) Distribute a copy of Worksheet 8.4 to each student. If time allows, choose a few students to read aloud the selection in the first part. If not, students should read it independently and answer the questions in the second part of the worksheet. Correct in class or collect when the lesson is finished.

Teaching Tip Substitution drills can be a good way to reinforce structures while practicing target vocabulary. Prompt students by cuing them with words or images.

Application 8.4 Note
In this activity, students will encounter unfamiliar words. If their meaning cannot be immediately extrapolated from the text, guide students though a reasoning process that leads to a better understanding of the selection. You can also ask the other students in the class if they have understood the word in question, and encourage those who have to assist their classmates.

Note: To allow for further review, Worksheet 8.5 may be assigned as homework.

Worksheet 8.1: Language Blast

Parts of the Body

DIRECTIONS Label the picture below using words from the word bank.

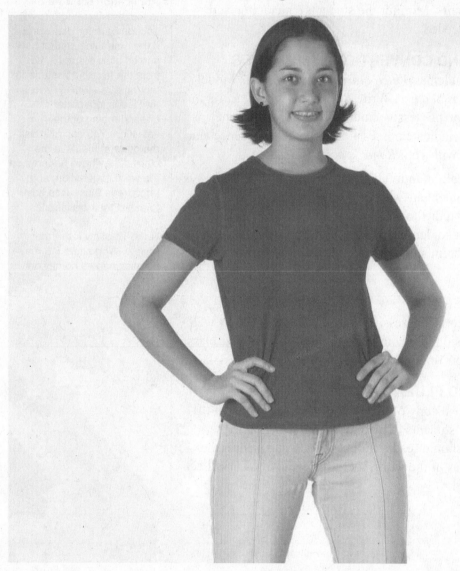

Word Bank

head	neck	chest	stomach	nose
eye	mouth	ear	arm	finger
leg	knee			

Name _____ Class _____ Date _____

Worksheet 8.2: Vocabulary Development

Image & Word Match

DIRECTIONS Match the classes with the pictures. Write the name of each class under the picture.

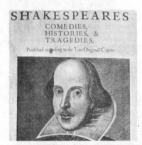

1. _____

2. _____

3. _____

4. _____

5. _____

6. _____

7. _____

Music	Physical Education	Language Arts
History	Science	Math
	Chemistry	

Worksheet 8.3: Speaking and Listening

Class Interviews

DIRECTIONS Interview four classmates about the classes they are taking. Write their answers in the spaces provided below. Then present your interviews. Remember to use proper subject and verb agreement.

Example: One of Sonia's classes is history. Math is Sonia's favorite class. She also likes her music class.

Classmate's name:	Classmate's name:	Classmate's name:	Classmate's name:

Worksheet 8.4: Reading and Fluency

Reading for Understanding

DIRECTIONS After you read the comic strip, read the sentences below. Circle
True or *False*. If the sentence is false, rewrite it to make it true.

1. Luis is studying at the café.   True   False

2. Luis is studying history and biology.   True   False

3. Luis has three exams on Friday.   True   False

4. James tells Luis the band needs a singer.   True   False

5. Luis says that he is not a singer.   True   False

6. The friends plan to practice on Tuesdays.   True   False

Worksheet 8.5: Daily Review

Crossword

DIRECTIONS Complete the following crossword puzzle using the clues and words from the word bank.

Across
1. You stand on these.
3. These are for walking.
8. You use these to hold things.
10. You can feel your heartbeat here.
11. This grows on top of your head.
12. Food goes here when you eat.

Down
2. You have these on each foot.
4. Used for listening.
5. You have these on each hand.
6. Used for speaking.
7. Holds up your head.
9. Used for chewing food and biting.

Word Bank

teeth	chest	ears	feet	mouth	fingers
stomach	toes	legs	hands	hair	neck

Lesson 9: Physical Characteristics

STEP 1: WORD DRILL *2 MINUTES*

(Teach/Guided Practice) Greet the class and say: *Today, I feel very tall!* As you say this, stretch tall in an exaggerated motion. Then say: *Sometimes, though, I feel _____*. Kneel down, miming being short. Encourage students to fill in with the word, *short*.

(Guided Practice) Continue by saying: *Today, I feel big*, acting out being big. Say: *Sometimes, though, I feel _____*. Act out being small and encourage the students to say the word, *small*. Say: *When I take a shower, I feel clean*, as you act out taking washing yourself and being happy. Say: *Sometimes, though, I feel _____*. Mime feeling dirty and encourage students to say the word, *dirty*. Help students to pronounce the vocabulary correctly. Ask for student volunteers to continue this game, using other antonym pairs of adjectives.

STEP 2: BUILD BACKGROUND *8 MINUTES*

(Teach/Guided Practice/Practice) This is a continuation of Step 1 to help students become more familiar with the vocabulary and the concept of adjectives. Write the vocabulary list and the short dialogue below on the board. Say: *I have a favorite movie star. She is pretty and tall*. Tell students that the words *pretty* and *tall* are adjectives, and that adjectives describe nouns. The words, *pretty* and *tall,* describe a person. Ask student for other adjectives they know. List examples on the board.

Go over the dialogue, teaching the phrase *favorite movie star*. Tell students they may choose any of the adjectives on the board, or others that they think of to fill in the blanks. Have students take turns reading parts A and B aloud, putting in different adjectives each time. Next, have partners practice the dialogue together. Circulate around the room and monitor pronunciation and word choice as students practice.

A: I have a favorite movie star.

B: Is your favorite movie star _____?

A: My favorite movie star is _____.

B: Is your favorite movie star _____?

A: My favorite movie star is _____.

B: I have a favorite movie star, too.

A: Tell me about your favorite movie star.

STEP 3: INDEPENDENT RECITATION *3 MINUTES*

(Apply) If students grasp Step 2 quickly, give them 2 minutes to memorize the dialogue. When time is up, erase the dialogue and chose a few students to recite it from memory in front of the class.

LESSON OBJECTIVES
Students will:

- recognize and correctly pronounce vocabulary words when reading aloud

- understand and learn how to use adjectives

- learn how to create phrases and sentences using adjectives correctly

- respond both verbally and in writing to questions with appropriate short phrases

- use vocabulary correctly during interactions with peers

- understand ordinal numbers

LESSON VOCABULARY
first, second, third, fourth, fifth, big, clean, dirty, small, long, short, tall, fat, thin, ugly, pretty

LESSON RESOURCES
Worksheet 9.1
Language Blast:
Ordinal Numbers

Worksheet 9.2
Vocabulary Development:
Matching

Worksheet 9.3
Speaking and Listening:
Cars, Cars, Cars

Worksheet 9.4
Reading and Fluency

Worksheet 9.5
Daily Review

Teaching Tip To reinforce the use of adjectives, point out and write examples of adjectives you use and students use throughout the day. See how many adjectives the class collects.

Note: To allow for further review, Worksheet 9.5 may be assigned as homework.

STEP 4: LANGUAGE BLAST *10 MINUTES*

(Teach/Guided Practice/Practice) Have five students line up. Count them: 1, 2, 3, 4, 5. Tell them that 1, 2, 3, 4 and 5 are cardinal, or counting numbers. Now point to each student in order, and say: *You are first. You are second. You are third. You are fourth. You are fifth.* Tell students that *first, second, third, fourth*, and *fifth* are ordinal numbers. They tell a place, or position. Pass out Worksheet 9.1 and review the ordinal numbers in the chart. Have students echo read with you as you point to each word and numeral. Next, read the directions for the calendar and questions with students. Do the first question together as a class. Then allow students approximately 10 minutes to complete the worksheet independently, and go over the answers as a class.

STEP 5: VOCABULARY DEVELOPMENT *10 MINUTES*

(Teach/Practice/Apply) Distribute Worksheet 9.2 and review the vocabulary and pictures. Read the directions aloud and complete one example, making sure students understand the concept of matching opposites. Have students work with partners to complete the exercise. When complete, review answers, asking students to read their answers out loud, correcting them as necessary.

STEP 6: GRAMMAR AND CONVENTIONS *15 MINUTES*

(Guided Practice) Say to students: *I like cars. Cars can be pretty. They can be big and long. They can be small and short. They can be clean. They can be dirty. I like _____ cars the best.* (fill in with your preference). Write each adjective you've used on the board. Ask students to list other adjectives that describe cars. Add these to the list.

SPEAKING AND LISTENING

(Practice/Apply) Distribute a copy of Worksheet 9.3 to each student. Read the directions aloud and choose two students to recite the dialogue, filling in the blanks with their own adjectives. After several students have recited the dialogue, divide students into pairs and have them continue to practice by trading roles to read each part.

STEP 7: READING AND FLUENCY *12 MINUTES*

(Apply/Review) Distribute Worksheet 9.4. Read the directions and select a few students to read the comic and questions aloud. Ask the class to complete the questions independently. Correct questions together and move on to Worksheet 9.5, which can be completed in class or assigned for homework.

Worksheet 9.1: Language Blast

Ordinal Numbers

DIRECTIONS Learn the vocabulary below with your teacher.

Ordinal Numbers

1st First	6th Sixth	11th Eleventh	16th Sixteenth	21st Twenty-first	26th Twenty-sixth
2nd Second	7th Seventh	12th Twelfth	17th Seventeenth	22nd Twenty-second	27th Twenty-seventh
3rd Third	8th Eighth	13th Thirteenth	18th Eighteenth	23rd Twenty-third	28th Twenty-eighth
4th Fourth	9th Ninth	14th Fourteenth	19th Nineteenth	24th Twenty-forth	29th Twenty-ninth
5th Fifth	10th Tenth	15th Fifteenth	20th Twentieth	25th Twenty-fifth	30th Thirtieth

DIRECTIONS Read the information in Paula's calendar and fill in the sentences below.

Sunday	Monday	Tuesday	Wednesday	Thursday	Friday	Saturday
1 date	2	3	4 exam	5	6	7 movie
8	9 my birthday!	10	11	12	13 doctor	14
15	16	17 haircut	18	19	20	21 party
22	23 dentist	24	25 paper due	26	27	28 skating

1. Paula has a date on the _____.

2. Her birthday is on the _____.

3. She has an exam on the _____.

4. Paula will see the doctor on the _____.

5. Paula's paper is due on the _____.

Worksheet 9.2: Vocabulary Development

Matching

DIRECTIONS Match the opposites in these two columns. Draw a line to join the opposites.

 big

 short

 clean

 pretty

 tall

 thin

 fat

 small

 ugly

 dirty

Worksheet 9.3: Speaking and Listening

Cars, Cars, Cars

DIRECTIONS Read this dialogue with a partner. Fill in the blanks using the adjectives in the word bank. When you are done, check your partner's answers and read the dialogue together. Then trade roles and read it again.

Word Bank

big	clean	dirty	small	ugly
short	tall	fat	pretty	thin

Student A: Doesn't that car look nice. Look at the stripes. I think it is very _____.

Student B: I think so, too. It only holds two people, though. It is too _____.

Student A: I like the car over there. It can hold many people. It is _____.

Student B: Yes, and it is also shiny and _____.

Student A: I wish I had a car like that. I would never let it get _____.

Student B: Me, too. I like cars. I like cars that are _____ and _____ and _____.

Worksheet 9.4: Reading and Fluency

Reading for Understanding

DIRECTIONS Read the story below and use it to help you with the exercise in second part of the worksheet.

DIRECTIONS Fill in the missing word in each sentence. Look at the dialogue above to help you.

1. Juan thinks the band is a lot _____.

2. They find a _____ outside the school.

3. The contest is called _____.

4. The prize money is $_____.

5. The contest is on _____.

6. Luis says "Let's get to _____!"

Worksheet 9.5: Daily Review

Word Search

DIRECTIONS Find the adjectives below in the word search puzzle. The words may appear horizontally, vertically, in regular order, backwards, or diagonally.

big	clean	dirty	small	long
	tall	fat	short	.

R	S	O	A	Z	F	M	L	P	S
T	B	D	L	T	A	L	L	C	R
F	O	I	U	A	N	O	A	D	E
R	S	M	G	F	E	N	M	T	N
W	O	C	R	K	R	G	S	A	I
N	S	D	L	O	M	W	D	S	H
L	H	P	R	E	T	T	Y	K	T
T	O	H	I	Y	A	S	L	O	N
E	R	H	E	O	L	N	G	P	M
Y	T	R	I	D	J	K	U	I	B

Lesson 10: Comparing Places Inside a School

STEP 1: WORD DRILL 2 *MINUTES*
(Teach/Guided Practice) Say to students: *This is our classroom.*
Gesture to students to repeat: *This is our classroom.* After the class has
repeated, say the sentence again and gesture for the class to repeat.

(Guided Practice) After the class has echoed, point to individual
students, say: *This is our classroom.* and invite the student to repeat
after you. Use this routine when introducing new words so that the
words are being pronounced correctly by everybody.

STEP 2: BUILD BACKGROUND 8 *MINUTES*
(Teach/Guided Practice/Practice) Write the short dialogue below on
the board. Read the first two lines aloud, and elicit repetition from the
students after each line. Go around the room and let each student have a
chance to speak. Continue with the rest of the dialogue, having students
repeat after you until they are comfortable pronouncing the words. Say
the first line (A), and have the class respond (B). Reverse roles. When
results are satisfactory, divide the class into pairs and allow them to
practice the routine for a few minutes while you circulate and monitor
progress. Have students name different places in the school as part of
the dialogue.

A: We need to talk. Let's talk in the gym.

B: The gym is too noisy. Where else can we talk?

A: Let's talk in the auditorium.

B: The auditorium is too noisy. Why don't we talk in the library?

A: No. We are not allowed to talk in the library.

B: Let's talk in the hall. I need to stop at my locker anyway.

STEP 3: INDEPENDENT RECITATION 3 *MINUTES*
(Apply) If students quickly grasp Step 2, give them two minutes to
memorize the dialogue on the board. When time is up, erase the
dialogue and chose a pairs to recite from memory in front of the class.

STEP 4: LANGUAGE BLAST 10 *MINUTES*
(Teach/Guided Practice/Practice) Draw an arrow on the board
pointing to students' left. Say: *left*, and gesture for students to repeat
left. Draw an arrow pointing right, say: *right*, and have students point
and repeat the word. Go over the direction words printed on Worksheet
10.1. Then go around the room and call on individual students. Ask:
Who is sitting to your left? and *Who is sitting to your right?* until each
student has answered at least one question. Distribute Worksheet 10.1
and allow students 5–10 minutes to complete it.

LESSON OBJECTIVES
Students will:

- respond to simple
  questions about different
  places at school
- learn comparatives and
  superlatives that compare
  different things
- speak in simple sentences
  to communicate directions
- use interrogative
  sentences to note
  differences between
  themselves and others
- listen to instructions and to
  their peers' dialogue

LESSON VOCABULARY
left, right, front, back, close,
far, behind, auditorium, gym,
library, cafeteria, hallway,
classroom, locker, office, big,
clean, dirty, small, long,
short, tall, fat, thin, ugly,
pretty, hot cold

LESSON RESOURCES
Worksheet 10.1
Language Blast:
Directions and Adjectives

Worksheet 10.2
Vocabulary Development:
Picture and Vocabulary
Match

Worksheet 10.3
Speaking and Listening:
Tell Me Something

Worksheet 10.4
Reading and Fluency

Worksheet 10.5
Daily Review

Teaching Tip Take students
on a school tour to introduce
them to school vocabulary
words, such as library,
auditorium, office, gym, and
so on.

STEP 5: VOCABULARY DEVELOPMENT *10 MINUTES*
(Teach/Practice/Apply) Distribute Worksheet 10.2. Begin by asking students if they recognize any of the pictures. Point to each word in the column on the right side of the page and pronounce it. Invite the class to repeat the vocabulary. Then ask students to complete the worksheet in pairs. Monitor the students' interaction and intervene if you hear incorrect pronunciation.

STEP 6: GRAMMAR AND CONVENTIONS *8 MINUTES*
(Guided Practice) Take two thick books of different sizes and set them beside your chair. Hold up the smaller of the two books and say: *This is a big book.* Have students repeat after you. Next, hold up the bigger book and say: *This is a bigger book.* Have students repeat after you. Hold up one of the books and gesture for students to say: *This is a big/bigger book.* Repeat until students are comfortable with the big/bigger distinction.

Now introduce a third book that is larger than the two. Say: *This is the biggest book.* Have students repeat after you. Go around the room and call on individual students. Hand the stack of books to one student and ask: *Which book is the biggest?* Help the student answer: *This is the biggest book.* and hold the book in the air. Repeat with other students. Write *big, bigger,* and *biggest* on the board and underline the comparative and superlative endings (*–er, –est*). Tell students that the comparative form compares two things. The superlative form compares three or more things. The regular comparative is formed by adding *–er* to the adjective, such as *bigger* (final consonants preceded by a vowel are doubled). The regular superlative is formed by adding the article *the* and the ending *–est.* As with the comparative, adjectives ending in final consonants preceded by vowel are doubled: *big—biggest.*

SPEAKING AND LISTENING
(Practice/Apply) To reinforce comparatives, superlatives and new vocabulary, distribute Worksheet 10.3 and ask the class to complete it in pairs. Correct it together.

STEP 7: READING AND FLUENCY *12 MINUTES*
(Apply/Review) Distribute a copy of Worksheet 10.4 to each student. If time allows, choose a few students to read aloud the selection in first part. If not, students should read independently and answer the follow-up questions in second part of the worksheet. Correct papers in class or collect them for correcting after the lesson is finished.

Optional Comparison Game
10–15 minutes
Photocopy the Comparison Game on page 155 and cut out the individual sentences. Make sure students feel comfortable pronouncing the vocabulary before starting. Distribute one sentence to each student. Ask: *Who is bigger than (provide the name of a student)* Have the student with the appropriate sentence answer: *I am bigger and then continue with than (name).* Then call for the student with the superlative sentence. This student says: *I am bigger than (name) and (the first student). I am the biggest.* Repeat using the other vocabulary words, making sure that most students get a turn.

Worksheet 10.4 Note
In this activity, students may encounter unfamiliar words. Encourage students to pair off and assist each other in completing the activity.

Note: To allow for further review, Worksheet 10.5 may be assigned as homework.

Worksheet 10.1: Language Blast

Directions and Adjectives

DIRECTIONS Review the direction words together as a class. Look at the seating plan below. With a partner, answer the questions about who sits next to whom. Remember that the front row is at the bottom of the seating plan.

Direction Words

left	right	front	back	close
	far	behind		

Antonio	Carla	Eno	Peri
Samad	Lia	Kendra	Jose
Chuy	Ana	Sara	Micah
Tito	Ahab	Kim	Ho

1. Who is sitting to Lia's left?

2. Who is sitting in front of Sara?

3. Who is sitting to Kendra's right?

4. Who is sitting behind Chuy?

5. Who is sitting in the front row?

6. Who is sitting in the back row?

7. Who is sitting close to Ana?

8. Who is sitting two seats in front of Eno?

9. Who is sitting far from Jose?

10. Who is sitting two seats to Carla's left?

Worksheet 10.2: Vocabulary Development

Picture and Vocabulary Match

DIRECTIONS Draw a line to match each word on the right with its picture on the left.

gym

library

cafeteria

hallway

classroom

locker

office

Worksheet 10.3: Speaking and Listening

Tell Me Something

DIRECTIONS Discuss the following questions among the members of your group. Be prepared for your teacher to ask you one or more of these questions in front of the class.

1. What is the biggest room in your school?

2. Who has the cleanest locker that you know?

3. Who is the tallest person in your family?

4. When is the coldest season of the year?

5. What is the smallest room in your school?

6. Who has the biggest feet in your group?

7. When is the hottest season of the year?

8. Who has the longest hair in your group?

9. Who has the smallest feet in your group?

10. Who has the shortest hair in your group?

Worksheet 10.4: Reading and Fluency

Reading for Understanding

DIRECTIONS Read the story below and use it to help you with the exercise in second part of the worksheet.

DIRECTIONS Read the sentences below. Circle the sentence or sentences in each pair that tell what is true.

1.   A. The band is waiting in the auditorium.

      B. Yolanda feels nervous.

2.   A. The band is waiting to play on stage.

      B. James does not feel well.

3.   A. Yolanda wants to talk in the library.
      B. The auditorium is too noisy.

4.   A. Luis thinks the other band sounds good.
      B. Yolanda thinks the other band sounds better than her band.

5.   A. James does not feel like going on stage.
      B. The band goes out on stage.

Worksheet 10.5: Daily Review

More or Less?

DIRECTIONS Write the correct comparative or superlative adjective to complete each sentence.

1. Tony's dog is the _____ (smaller/smallest) dog I have ever seen.

2. Pedro is _____ (shorter/shortest) than Carlos.

3. Keisha is the _____ (taller/tallest) girl I know.

4. The gym is the _____ (bigger/biggest) room in the school.

5. The library is _____ (bigger/biggest) than the hallway.

6. I live _____ (closer/closest) to the school than Julio does.

7. Ms. Hernandez has a _____ (louder/loudest) voice than Ms. Gordon.

8. My locker is _____ (cleaner/cleanest) than Ramon's.

9. My brother has the _____ (dirtier/dirtiest) room I have ever seen!

10. The lunchroom is _____ (smaller/smallest) than the auditorium.

Lesson 11: Describing Yourself and Others

STEP 1: WORD DRILL *2 MINUTES*
(Teach/Guided Practice) Greet the class with a smile. Point to yourself and, using an expressive tone, say: *I am happy.* Gesture to the class to model your smile, point to themselves, and repeat: *I am happy.* While students remain smiling, point to a member of the class and say: *She is happy.* Then point to another member of the class and say: *He is happy.* Have students point to another member of the class and repeat: *She is happy.* or *He is happy.* Then have students look at one another and say: *You are happy.* Next pout or frown and point to yourself and say: *I am sad.* Gesture for students to mimic your facial expression and repeat: *I am sad.* Have students point to each other while continuing to pout or frown. Have students say: *He is sad.* or *She is sad.*

(Guided Practice) After students have echoed as a class, call on random students, smile, and ask: *What am I?* Students should point to you and respond: *You are happy.* Call on other students, pout, and ask: *What am I?* Students should point to you and respond: *You are sad.* Use this routine when introducing new words to keep the students involved.

STEP 2: BUILD BACKGROUND *8 MINUTES*
(Teach/Guided Practice/Practice) This is a continuation of the word drill and can be used to describe self or others. Write the dialogue below on the board, read the first two lines aloud, and elicit repetition from the students after each line. Let each student practice describing another student, as well as him- or herself, starting the dialogue from the beginning each time. Have students repeat the dialogue until they are comfortable pronouncing the words. Then say the first line (A) and prompt the class to respond (B). Reverse roles. When it seems that students fully comprehend the dialogue and can pronounce all words, allow students to practice the new routine in pairs while you circulate and monitor progress.

A: I am frowning. What am I?
B: You are sad.
A: I am smiling. What am I?
B: You are happy.
A: You are smiling. What are you?
B: I am happy, too.

STEP 3: INDEPENDENT RECITATION *3 MINUTES*
(Apply) Give students two minutes to memorize the dialogue on the board. When time is up, erase the dialogue, and choose a few pairs to recite from memory in front of the class.

LESSON OBJECTIVES
Students will:

- respond to basic questions using short phrases and complete sentences
- learn vocabulary related to social greetings and introductions
- use gestures and other methods of unspoken communication to learn new words
- learn adjectives used to describe oneself as well as other people
- speak using proper pronunciation of vocabulary words
- use comparatives with the words *more* and *most* to describe others
- listen to, understand, and follow both written and oral instructions
- listen to and respond to peers as they describe themselves and others

LESSON VOCABULARY
intelligent, stupid, interesting, dull, funny, talkative, nervous, energetic, hopeful, elegant, stylish, frightened, playful, loving, happy, sad, upset, excited

LESSON RESOURCES
Worksheet 11.1
Language Blast: Adjectives

Worksheet 11.2
Vocabulary Development: Tell Me More

Worksheet 11.3
Speaking and Listening: My Family

Worksheet 11.4
Reading and Fluency

Worksheet 11.5
Daily Review

STEP 4: LANGUAGE BLAST *10 MINUTES*
(Teach/Guided Practice/Practice) Ask students what words they know to describe themselves or others. (*funny*, *tall*, *short*) Then pass out Worksheet 11.1 and teach the vocabulary on the worksheet. Explain to students that each picture on the worksheet shows a word that describes a person. Point to each picture and pronounce the word for students. Have students repeat the words as you say them. Mimic the facial expression as you say each word, and gesture for students to do the same. Ask volunteers if the words they offer describe themselves or someone they know. Allow students 5 minutes to complete Worksheet 11.1. Then ask volunteers to share their answers.

STEP 5: VOCABULARY DEVELOPMENT *10 MINUTES*
(Teach/Practice/Apply) Distribute a copy of Worksheet 11.2 to each student. Point out that the pictures and vocabulary words are the same as those on Worksheet 11.1. Show students the comparative and superlative example on the worksheet (*more exciting, most exciting*). Ask students to remember what they learned about comparatives and superlatives in Lesson 10. Tell them that they will practice using multi-syllabic comparatives and superlatives.

Review syllables by sharing the following words and asking students to tell how many syllables they hear in each: *sad (one), happy (two), excite (two), exciting (three).*

Remind students that a *comparative* is a word that is used to compare two things. A comparative is formed by adding *-er* to the end of a descriptive word, or by using the word *more* before the descriptive word. Then remind students that a *superlative* is a word used to compare more than two things. A superlative is formed by adding *–est* to the end of a descriptive word, or by using the word *most* before the descriptive word.

Write the word *intelligent* on the board. Say the word and have students tell how many syllables they hear (four). Then write these words under it: *intelligenter, more intelligent, intelligentest,* and *most intelligent.* Ask students to say each word aloud. Ask students to identify which comparative and superlative forms sound correct (*more intelligent; most intelligent.*)

Remind students that the word *than* often occurs in comparatives. Write the following example: *A day is _____ than a week.* Ask students for a word that completes the sentence frame. (*shorter*) Ask a volunteer to write the complete sentence on the board: *A day is shorter than a week.*

Teaching Tip Model facial expressions that correspond to the personality traits. Use facial expressions and an expressive tone in the dialogue to help students identify each trait.

Optional Guessing Game: What Am I?
10-15 minutes
Photocopy a few copies of the Game 5 board on page 156. Cut out the adjectives and hold up each one for students to review meanings and pronunciations before playing the game. Then put masking tape on the back of each adjective and stick it to a student's forehead. (Students must not know which adjective they "wear" on their heads.) Tell students to travel around the room, asking each other questions to help them guess which word they have. Examples: Do I talk a lot? If the answer is yes, Am I talkative? Do I like to play? Am I exciting? Circulate and listen to the way students are asking and answering questions. You might give the first few students who guess their words small prizes.

Application 11.3 Note
Allowing students to correct each other and explain the corrections gives you the opportunity to check students' comprehension of material being taught. It also gives students a chance to use and reinforce vocabulary and grammar concepts being taught—by assisting others or by listening to and responding to assistance from others.

Note: To allow for further review, Worksheet 11.5 may be assigned as homework.

Have students complete Worksheet 11.2. When students have finished, ask volunteers to read a sentence or two aloud, having the class repeat each sentence. Listen to student pronunciations as they repeat, and correct pronunciation as necessary.

STEP 6: GRAMMAR AND CONVENTIONS *15 MINUTES*
(Guided Practice) Read aloud the script at the bottom of Worksheet 11.3 as students listen. Speak slowly and clearly. Then read the script again as students look at the listening comprehension questions as you read. When you are done, have students complete the multiple-choice questions on their worksheets.

SPEAKING AND LISTENING
(Practice/Apply) After students have completed their worksheets, have individual students share their answers with the class. If students answer incorrectly, call on a volunteer to tell why the answer is incorrect and to supply the correct answer, referring to the text as proof.

STEP 7: READING AND FLUENCY *12 MINUTES*
(Apply/Review) Distribute Worksheet 11.4. Choose a student to read aloud the selection in the first part of the worksheet. Explain any new language to students. Then have students answer the reading comprehension questions in the second part of the worksheet. Correct the answers in class or collect papers and correct them when the lesson is finished.

Worksheet 11.1: Language Blast

Adjectives

DIRECTIONS Review each of the vocabulary words. Then choose one vocabulary word to complete each of the sentences below.

 funny

 interesting

 nervous

 energetic

 hopeful

 elegant

 stylish

 frightened

 playful

 loving

1. I am _____.

2. I am not _____.

3. My best friend is _____.

4. My best friend is not _____.

5. My mother or father is _____.

6. My mother or father is not _____.

Worksheet 11.2: Vocabulary Development

Tell Me More

DIRECTIONS Complete each of the sentences below with the comparative or superlative form of the adjective that appears in parentheses.

1. The movie was _____ than the book (funny).

2. I am _____ about the test than you are. (nervous)

3. Lisa's dad is _____ than her mom. (talkative)

4. The restaurant was _____ than the diner. (elegant)

5. The museum was _____ than the library. (interesting)

6. My brother is _____ person I know. (intelligent)

7. The brown dog is the _____ of all the dogs on the street. (playful)

8. My best friend is the _____ of all of my friends. (stylish)

9. My sister is _____ than I am. (energetic)

Worksheet 11.3: Speaking and Listening

My Family

DIRECTIONS Listen to the script as your teacher reads it to you. Then answer the listening comprehension questions below.

1. Who is the oldest child in Marco's family?
   A. Kim
   B. Rosa

2. Which word best describes Kim?
   A. energetic
   B. stylish

3. Which pet is more playful?
   A. Charlie
   B. Sunny

4. Which word best describes Marco?
   A. talkative
   B. dull

5. Who gets nervous?
   A. Marco's parents
   B. Marco's sisters

6. Whose family is more interesting?
   A. Patrick's family
   B. Marco's family

7. Who is Kim is funnier than?

   A. Rosa
   B. Marco

8. What does Marco hope his family continues to be?

   A. loving
   B. funny

DIRECTIONS Read the script to students, speaking clearly and slowly. Tell students that they may take notes as they listen.

My name is Marco. I live with my parents and two sisters. We are the most interesting family I know. Rosa is older than I am. She is funny, but my little sister Kim is funnier than Rosa. Kim is the youngest child in my family. She is very energetic, which sometimes makes my parents nervous. She is less talkative than Rosa, but more talkative than I am. My sisters are both intelligent, but I think I am the most intelligent of my siblings. My best friend Patrick is more intelligent than I. His family is less interesting than my family because there are no siblings. Patrick has a dog named Charlie, who is very playful. Charlie is more playful than my goldfish Sunny. In fact, my goldfish is a dull pet. Someday, I hope to have a dog.

Worksheet 11.4: Reading and Fluency

Reading for Understanding

DIRECTIONS Read the postcard below.

Sedna Kanut
123 Main St.
Juneau, AK 99850

Dear Sedna,
I am writing to you from Mexico! It is much warmer here than it is in Alaska. I am very
happy to be here, but I think my brother Chu is happier than I. He was frightened on the
plane, so I played games with him until he was less nervous. The scenery here is beautiful
and colorful. Alaska is also beautiful, but it is duller than Mexico. The people here are very
interesting. They are funny and talkative. Their clothing is more stylish than the clothes we
wear in Alaska. I will be sad when we leave, but I think my mother will be the saddest of
all. I will be excited to come home and see you! I hope you are having fun!
From,
Anana

DIRECTIONS Read each sentence. Think about what you read. If the sentence
is true, write *True* on the line. If the sentence is false, rewrite the sentence to
make it true.

1. Anana was frightened on the plane.

_____

2. The people in Mexico are interesting.

_____

3. The scenery in Mexico is duller than the scenery in Alaska.

_____

4. Chu will be the saddest when they leave Mexico.

_____

5. Mexico is warmer than Alaska.

_____

Worksheet 11.5: Daily Review

Weather

DIRECTIONS Read the weather forecasts and answer the questions that
follow. Write in complete sentences.

WEATHER FORECASTS	
San Francisco, CALIFORNIA	**Rio de Janeiro, BRAZIL**
High Temperature – **59 degrees F** Low Temperature – **48 degrees F** **Today** Cloudy with short periods of sun. Winds at 5 to 10 miles per hour. Chance of rain 20 percent. **Tonight** Clear and cool. Winds at 5 miles per hour. Chance of rain 5 percent.	High Temperature – **75 degrees F** Low Temperature – **66 degrees F** **Today** Sunny with light rain and thunderstorms. Winds at 10 to 15 miles per hour. Chance of rain 80 percent. **Tonight** Evening showers. Winds at 5 to 10 miles per hour. Chance of rain 60 percent.

1. Is Rio de Janeiro warmer than San Francisco?

_____

2. Is San Francisco cloudier than Rio de Janeiro?

_____

3. Is it windier in San Francisco or Rio de Janeiro?

_____

4. Does Rio de Janeiro have more rain than San Francisco?

_____

5. Is San Francisco cooler at night than Rio de Janeiro?

_____

Lesson 12: Plans for the Weekend

STEP 1: WORD DRILL *2 MINUTES*

(Teach/Guided Practice) Greet the class, and say: *I have plans for the weekend. I am going to go to the mall.* Have students repeat the sentences after you. Then say: *I am going to go shopping at the mall.* Again, ask students to repeat what you have said. Then say: *I am going to go to many places.*

(Guided Practice) Point to individual students and have them repeat what you say. Introduce a new vocabulary word with each sentence: *I have plans this weekend. I am going to a friend's house.* or *I have plans this weekend. I am going to see a movie.* Pantomime, draw, or show pictures of the activities to make the meaning clear. As students repeat each sentence, pay attention to their pronunciation and correct it, if necessary. Encourage quiet students to speak loudly and clearly.

STEP 2: BUILD BACKGROUND *8 MINUTES*

(Teach/Guided Practice/Practice) Encourage students to practice speaking about their weekend plans by following the short dialogue below. Write the dialogue on the board and read the first two lines aloud to students, using an expressive voice. Gesture for students to repeat as you read each line. Repeat until students are comfortable pronouncing the words. Let each student practice telling about their weekend plans, starting the dialogue from the beginning each time. After each student has had a turn, continue with the remaining four lines of the dialogue. Repeat until students are comfortable pronouncing the words. Then say the first line (A) and ask the class to respond by reading the second line (B). When the class seems comfortable with the new vocabulary words in the dialogue, have students practice the entire dialogue with a partner. Each partner should take a turn reading the A role and the B role. Walk around the room as students practice the dialogue, listening for and correcting pronunciation, as needed.

A: Do you have plans this weekend?
B: Yes, I have plans this weekend. I am going to go to a friend's house.
A: I also have plans this weekend.
B: Where are you going to go?
A: I am going to see a movie.
B: I am going to study with my friend.

STEP 3: INDEPENDENT RECITATION *3 MINUTES*

(Apply) Ask students who are doing well with the dialogue to turn their away from the board and recite the dialogue from memory in front of the class. If students have trouble remembering the dialogue, allow them to glance over their shoulders at the board before continuing the recitation.

LESSON OBJECTIVES
Students will:
- understand basic phrases about plans and actions
- use short phrases or sentences in social settings
- use simple vocabulary to convey basic needs
- use comparatives and superlatives to identify their ideas and actions
- listen to instructions and to their peers' dialogue

LESSON VOCABULARY
taller, tallest, going to see, going to go, going to dance, going to go shopping, the mall, a club, a friend's house, downtown, the beach, the movies, a café

LESSON RESOURCES
Worksheet 12.1
Language Blast: Word Search

Worksheet 12.2
Vocabulary Development: Places to Go

Worksheet 12.3
Speaking and Listening: What Are You Doing?

Worksheet 12.4
Reading and Fluency

Worksheet 12.5
Daily Review

Teaching Tip During the word drill, encourage students to talk about where they are going or would like to go. Ask them to elaborate on what they plan to do at their destination. Try to get them excited about their plans. That excitement will help them absorb the new lesson.

Note: If you need more time for the lesson, you may assign Worksheet 12.5 as homework.

STEP 4: LANGUAGE BLAST *10 MINUTES*

(Teach/Guided Practice/Practice) To teach the comparatives and superlatives, have two student volunteers of different heights come to the front of the class. Point to the shorter student and say: *(student) is tall.* Then point to the taller student and say: *(student) is taller.* Gesture to indicate the height differences. Write both sentences on the board. Circle the *–er* ending at the end of the comparative and explain that we can add *–er* to show the difference. Ask a third student, of a different height, to come to the front of the class. Repeat to teach the superlative form of *–est.* Model other examples with the class with different adjectives. Point out any spelling changes that occur when adding *–er* or *–est.* Preteach any adjectives, as necessary. Pass out Worksheet 12.1 and allow students 5–10 minutes to complete it.

STEP 5: VOCABULARY DEVELOPMENT *10 MINUTES*

(Teach/Practice/Apply) Distribute a copy of Worksheet 12.2 to each student and read it as a class. Ask students if they know any of the vocabulary words on the left. Ask them if they can identify any of the images. Encourage students to explain, or even act out, the meanings of these phrases. For example, a student trying to describe *eat dinner* might pretend he or she has a plate of food and is using a fork to eat. Read each place name aloud and have the students repeat after you. Then, read aloud each of the phrases on the right side. Pantomime or draw each activity to demonstrate the meaning. After each phrase, ask the students if they like each activity. Encourage them to identify with whom they do each activity, how often, or any other information about the activity.

STEP 6: GRAMMAR AND CONVENTIONS *15 MINUTES*

(Guided Practice) Draw a week calendar on the board. Mark an *X* on today's day. Say to the students: *Today is (day). I have plans for the weekend.* Point to Saturday and Sunday. Say: *This weekend I'm going to see a movie.* Underline *I'm going to* in the sentence and circle *see.* Explain to students that we use the present tense of the verb *be* with *going to* and a verb to talk about the future. Model several examples with the students. Ask students to tell you something they are going to do this weekend.

SPEAKING AND LISTENING

(Practice/Apply) To reinforce the future tense with *going to* and to help students learn the vocabulary, pass out Worksheet 12.3. Have the students write sentences about what they are going to do this weekend using the responses from 12.2. Model an example with the class. Then, have students ask three classmates what they are going to do tomorrow and write the responses. Have the class share information about their classmates' plans.

STEP 7: READING AND FLUENCY *12 MINUTES*

(Apply/Review) Distribute a copy of Worksheet 12.4 to each student. Explain that the worksheet shows a postcard; ask if any students have ever sent or received a postcard. Then, have a student read each line of the postcard. Help the students with any challenging words. Have the students answer the questions. Correct the worksheet in class, or collect it when the lesson is complete.

Worksheet 12.1: Language Blast

Word Search

DIRECTIONS Find these comparatives and superlatives on the word search.

bigger biggest	dirtier dirtiest	smallest smaller
tallest taller	longer longest	fatter fattest
ugliest uglier	prettier prettiest	cleaner cleanest
shorter shortest		

F	D	I	R	T	I	E	R	X	W	Q	F	V	A	G	M	W	A	B	X
W	N	L	O	U	E	W	A	B	B	T	A	L	L	E	R	B	J	D	H
X	S	G	W	S	C	J	T	I	K	A	W	D	B	N	D	P	Q	T	U
D	X	M	O	J	W	E	U	G	N	L	H	W	I	A	H	R	K	Y	O
F	G	F	M	C	H	S	K	G	L	L	R	A	F	R	Q	E	C	S	N
S	M	A	L	L	E	S	T	E	L	E	S	E	M	N	T	T	K	F	H
Q	D	T	V	M	N	K	T	S	G	I	S	F	J	F	D	T	E	D	K
D	E	T	B	F	B	E	K	T	X	Z	E	F	B	O	S	I	E	Y	I
O	C	E	R	I	U	Z	O	Q	G	V	C	S	G	U	Z	E	B	R	J
R	O	S	B	O	L	C	L	E	A	N	E	S	T	Y	E	R	F	R	D
I	N	T	I	N	A	O	N	A	S	D	E	B	F	I	R	J	M	I	U
C	S	E	G	M	R	L	K	C	O	M	R	O	N	I	S	I	N	S	A
L	O	N	G	E	R	G	C	A	N	A	A	E	T	G	U	D	E	T	N
E	U	Q	E	R	A	A	D	N	M	H	Y	L	A	B	O	I	T	S	F
A	I	P	R	E	T	T	I	E	S	T	H	R	L	I	O	R	I	E	A
N	T	E	T	H	R	U	G	L	I	E	R	G	L	E	T	T	A	T	T
E	L	I	V	E	E	V	N	I	R	T	D	T	E	I	R	I	U	R	T
R	O	N	S	L	O	N	G	E	S	T	B	S	S	E	C	E	S	O	E
A	N	D	I	M	D	O	L	P	I	A	N	A	T	N	N	S	T	H	R
U	N	S	H	O	R	T	E	R	S	N	D	E	B	T	A	T	F	S	X

Worksheet 12.2: Vocabulary Development

Places to Go

DIRECTIONS Look at the first and second columns. These are different kinds of places to visit. In the third column, there are many things that people do. Match each place with the things that people do there. There may be more than one answer possible. Write your answers on the lines below.

1. mall

A. see a movie

B. go out with friends

2. café

C. eat dinner

D. go shopping

E. have coffee

3. friend's house

F. read a book

G. hang out

H. dance

4. downtown

I. go swimming

J. watch TV

5. the beach

1. _____ _____ _____

2. _____ _____ _____

3. _____ _____ _____

4. _____ _____ _____

5. _____ _____ _____

Name _____ Class _____ Date_____

What Are You Doing?

DIRECTIONS Use your new vocabulary words to write sentences. Write about what you might want to do this weekend. Use the words below. Be sure to answer in complete sentences.

What are you going to do this weekend?

1. _____ (mall)

2. _____ (café)

3. _____ (friend's house)

4. _____ (downtown)

5. _____ (the beach)

DIRECTIONS Now ask three people in your class what they are going to do tomorrow. Write their responses below.

6. _____

7. _____

8. _____

Worksheet 12.4: Reading and Fluency

Reading for Understanding

DIRECTIONS **Read this postcard from Alaska.**

Dear Erin, I was so glad to hear about your trip to Mexico! It sounds like you are having the greatest trip ever. You're right about it being colder in Alaska—it's one of the coldest places around. Mexico is probably one of the warmest. I don't think Alaska is dull, though. We have some great malls and cafés downtown. They are not too far from our house. The Sailor's Shanty café is closest to our house, and it is my favorite. They serve the biggest and tastiest french fries around. I went to my friend's house yesterday and we were talking about your trip. We looked at Mexico on the map. You went much farther than I have ever gone—and I bet you have sunnier beaches there, too! Your pal, Samantha	To: Erin Decker 321 Calle Ancha Mexico City, Mexico

DIRECTIONS **Answer these questions about the postcard.**

1. What does Samantha think about the Sailor's Shanty café?

_____

2. How is Mexico different from Alaska?

_____

3. What food does Samantha like to eat?

_____

4. Which places does Samantha enjoy going to?

_____

5. What does Erin think about Alaska?

_____

Worksheet 12.5: Daily Review

Vacation

DIRECTIONS Imagine you are on vacation and you want to write to a friend about the place you are visiting. Write to your friend to tell him or her about the place and your plans during your vacation. You can tell your friend about something fun you have done or want to do. Write your friend on the postcard below. Be sure to use the vocabulary words and write in complete sentences.

To My Friend

Lesson 13: Life Predictions and Spontaneous Decisions

STEP 1: WORD DRILL 2 *MINUTES*
(Teach/Guided Practice) Write the words *yesterday*, *today*, and *tomorrow* on the board. Draw arrows from *yesterday* to *today* and from *today* to *tomorrow*. Write the words *past* under *yesterday*, *present* under *today*, and *future* under *tomorrow*. Circle the word *future*. Tell students that tomorrow is in the future. Say: *future* aloud. Ask the students to repeat the word. Ask students: *What will you do tomorrow?* (I will go to school. I will sleep late. I will see a friend.)

(Guided Practice) After students have echoed the words several times, point to the word *today*. Explain that *today* is happening right now. It is the *present*. Point to the word *yesterday*. Tell students that yesterday has already happened. It is the *past*. Point to *tomorrow* and *future*. Tell students that *tomorrow* has not yet happened. It is the *future*. Explain that we do not know what will happen in the future. We can only guess what might happen. When we make a guess about a future event we use phrases like *I think I will* or *I think they will* to describe our prediction.

STEP 2: BUILD BACKGROUND 8 *MINUTES*
(Teach/Guided Practice/Practice) Use a calendar to help students understand the concepts of *past*, *present*, and *future*. This will help students understand how to make predictions about future events. Hold up the calendar. Point to today's date. Say: *present*. Ask the students to repeat the word with you. Point to yesterday's date and say: *past,* and have the students echo you. Point to tomorrow's date and say: *future*. Students should repeat the word with you. Flip the calendar to show the previous month. Say: *This month is in the past*. Flip the calendar to the month before that. Ask: *Is this month in the past?* Wait for students to respond.

Flip the calendar one month ahead. Say: *This month is in the future*. Ask students to repeat the sentence with you. Circle an upcoming holiday or school event on the calendar. Say: *On (Memorial Day), I think I will (go to a party)*. Explain that using the phrase *I think I will...* shows that you are predicting or guessing what you might do in the future. Ask students to think of things that they will do in the future. Encourage students to use the following sentence frames:

During the summer, I think I will _____.

For my birthday, I think I will _____.

Next weekend, I think I will _____.

LESSON OBJECTIVES
Students will:

- learn the concepts of past, present, and future

- learn how to use the simple future form to talk about events in the future

- respond with appropriate short phrases or sentences to answer questions about future events

- use comparatives and superlatives to compare people, places, and things

- carefully follow instructions and listen to feedback from peers

LESSON VOCABULARY
I think I will...have kids, get married, be a (doctor), go to college, buy a house or apartment, live in (California), have a family, get a job, live in a different country, travel around the world, start my own business, write a book, direct a movie, be on TV.

LESSON RESOURCES
Worksheet 13.1
Language Blast: Comparatives and Superlatives

Worksheet 13.2
Vocabulary Development: I Think I Will…

Worksheet 13.3
Speaking and Listening: Using the Simple Future Form

Worksheet 13.4
Reading and Fluency

Worksheet 13.5
Daily Review

STEP 3: INDEPENDENT RECITATION *3 MINUTES*

(Apply) If students understand Step 2, have them tell partners what job they would like to have in the future. Then call on volunteers to tell the class how their partners responded. Encourage students to use the following sentence frame. In the future, (student's name) thinks he/she will be a (job).

STEP 4: LANGUAGE BLAST *10 MINUTES*

(Teach/Guided Practice/Practice) Explain that comparatives are words that compare two things. Superlatives are words that compare three or more things. Write the following sentences on the board:

Ben is tall. Ben is taller than Samad.

Circle the word *taller*. Explain to students that *taller* is a comparative form because it compares two people. Ask students for other words that compare two things (softer, smaller, higher, harder, richer, more exciting). Write a few of the words on the board. Write the following sentence on the board to help students understand superlatives:

Ben is the tallest kid in our class.

Circle the word *tallest*. Explain that the word *tallest* compares Ben to all the students in class. *Tallest* ends in *–est,* which is the superlative form. Have volunteers think of words that are superlatives (most happy, funniest, highest, loudest).

Pass out Worksheet 13.1. Explain that comparatives and superlatives can be divided into three categories: *looks*, such as height and size; *acts*, such as friendly or shy; and *feels*, such as happy or angry. Draw a three-column chart with these traits as headings on the board. Have students think of actors they know from TV or the movies. Ask them to think of words to describe these actors, then write the words on the board as students offer them. Encourage students to complete the chart, then write sentences about these celebrities using the comparatives and superlatives from the chart.

STEP 5: VOCABULARY DEVELOPMENT *10 MINUTES*

(Teach/Practice/Apply) Distribute Worksheet 13.2. Ask students to describe each picture. Call attention to vocabulary words that are related to the pictures. Have students match captions to pictures, then check the pictures they think apply to their own futures. Ask students to think of other words and ideas that may also apply.

STEP 6: GRAMMAR AND CONVENTIONS *15 MINUTES*

(Guided Practice) Ask the class: *What will you do tomorrow?* Explain that when talking about the future, we use the phrase *I will*. This is the simple future form. Model sentences for students, such as:

Tomorrow, I will (teach a class, go shopping, see my friend).
Have each student tell about one thing they will do tomorrow. Remind students that sometimes we do not know what we will do in the future. Then we say: *I think I will* when we are guessing what we will do.

Teaching Tip Use a calendar of the days of the month to explain the concepts of past, present, and future. Write the days of the week and have students identify the day that is *present,* name a day that is *past,* and name a day that is in the *future.*

Worksheet 13.4 Note
In this activity, students will encounter unfamiliar words. If students need help, draw a picture of a word or mime its meaning. Encourage other students to help those who are having difficulty.

Note: To allow for further review, Worksheet 13.5 may be assigned as homework.

SPEAKING AND LISTENING

(Practice/Apply) To help students better understand the simple future tense, write the following dialogue on the board.

Carlos: What are you going to do on Saturday?

Harriet: I am going to visit my grandparents.

Circle *are you going to do* and *am going to visit* in these sentences. Explain that these sentences use the simple future form. Ask students to complete Worksheet 13.3. When students are finished, have volunteers read aloud their dialogues. Discuss any questions students may have before moving on to Worksheet 13.4.

STEP 7: READING AND FLUENCY 12 *MINUTES*

(Apply/Review) Distribute Worksheet 13.4. If time allows, choose a few students to read aloud the selection in the first part of the worksheet. If not, students should read it independently and answer the follow-up questions in the second part. Correct papers in class or collect them to correct when the lesson is finished.

Worksheet 13.1: Language Blast

Comparatives and Superlatives

DIRECTIONS Think of your favorite actor. What kinds of words could you use to describe him or her? Write the words in each column.

Looks	Acts	Feels

DIRECTIONS On the lines below, write sentences that compare your actor with other actors chosen by the class. Use comparatives and superlatives in your sentences.

_____

_____

_____

_____

_____

_____

_____

Worksheet 13.2: Vocabulary Development

I Think I Will...

DIRECTIONS Look at the pictures and captions. Write the letter of the picture that belongs with each caption. Then check the pictures that show what is in *your* future.

A

1. I think I will...get married. _____

B

2. I think I will... go to college. _____

C

3. I think I will... travel the world. _____

D

4. I think I will... own my own business. _____

DIRECTIONS Look at the pictures you checked. Then answer the question below.

What will you do when you are older?

_____.

Worksheet 13.3: Speaking and Listening

Using the Simple Future Form

DIRECTIONS Choose words and phrases from the word bank to complete the dialogue below.

Word Bank

I'll come	are you doing	starts
I will	am going to see	I'll
let's meet	are you going	are you going

1A: Hi. What _____ tonight?

1B: I _____ a movie with my friend.

2A: Great! _____ with you.

2B: _____ to bring your friend, too?

3A: Yes, I think _____. What time _____ to get there?

3B: The film _____ at 8:30, so _____ outside at 8:15.

4A: Great. _____ be there.

Worksheet 13.4: Reading and Fluency

Reading for Understanding

DIRECTIONS Read the following flier.

CLEAN AIR CLUB MEETING

The Clean Air Club will meet on Saturday, March 1st. We are going to plant trees at City Center.

Will you join us?

We will meet in the school lunchroom at 9 o'clock. We will leave for City Center at 9:30.

After planting, we are going to have lunch at Pete's Café.

Come one, come all! Planting trees is the greatest way to spend a Saturday!

HELP OUR PLANET. DO YOUR PART!

DIRECTIONS Read each sentence and underline the correct answer.

1. According to the flier, the Clean Air Club is going to plant trees at the (school / City Center).

2. The Clean Air Club will leave for the City Center at (9 o'clock / 9:30).

3. After planting trees, club members will (leave / eat lunch at) Pete's Café.

4. According to the flier, planting trees is the (better / best) way to spend a Saturday.

5. The Clean Air Club wants to (eat lunch/help our planet).

Worksheet 13.5: Daily Review

Make Your Own Flier

DIRECTIONS Think about a club you are in, or an activity you care about.
Make a flier to invite people to join.

Think of an event at school. It could be real or imagined. It could be a play. It could be a bake sale. It could be champion sports game. Use the space below to make a flier. Your flier should tell the date, the time, and the place of the event. It should tell why it is special. It should get people interested in being there.

_____

_____

_____

_____

_____

_____

_____

_____

_____

_____

_____

Lesson 14: Lost in the City

STEP 1: WORD DRILL 2 *MINUTES*
(Teach/Guided Practice) Gather pictures of a restaurant, library, shopping center, bank, or other building or place listed in the vocabulary. Hold up each picture, one at a time, and say the name of the vocabulary word. Encourage students to repeat the name and, if possible, tell its purpose. Write vocabulary words on the board and ask students to say each word and perform an action that is related to the place or building. For example, *eating* to suggest the word *restaurant; counting change* to suggest *bank.*

(Guided Practice) Once you have finished introducing each building and name, ask individual students to recite the names and point to the pictures that match. This helps students internalize the new vocabulary. Write the following sentence frames on the board and have students supply the correct place in each.

1. I eat in a _____. (restaurant)
2. I get medicine at a _____. (pharmacy)
3. I buy clothes at a _____. (shopping center)
4. I get stamps at the _____. (post office)
5. I borrow books from the _____. (library)
6. I take out money from the _____. (bank)
7. I see a movie in the _____. (movie theater)
8. When I travel I wait at the _____ (bus stop)

STEP 2: BUILD BACKGROUND 8 *MINUTES*
(Teach/Guided Practice/Practice) Once Step 1 is complete and students are familiar with the different kinds of buildings, try this exercise. Ask students to name a place they have visited and tell what they did there. Then ask them to name a place they have not yet been to and tell what they will do if they go there. Have students choose the names of places from the vocabulary to complete the sentence frames below on separate sheets of paper:

1. I once went to a _____. I _____ there.
2. If I go to a _____, I will _____ there. When students have had a chance to respond, call on volunteers to read aloud their answers. Write a few responses on the board and have the class echo read them with you.

STEP 3: INDEPENDENT RECITATION 3 *MINUTES*
(Apply) Write the vocabulary words on the board and have students create new sentences using the words. For example, *I have never been to town hal* or *I like to eat in restaurants.*

LESSON OBJECTIVES
Students will:
- ask and answer basic questions used in social settings
- use simple vocabulary to express location
- read simple texts and respond to questions
- show understanding of instructions and other information with nonverbal responses
- understand and use simple prepositions of place

LESSON VOCABULARY
bank, post office, movie theater, restaurant, town hall, library, shopping center, pharmacy, bus stop, supermarket, stadium, hotel, train station, café, hospital, museum, in, on, at, over, under, behind, in front of, beside, to the left, to the right, across from, around

LESSON RESOURCES

Worksheet 14.1
Language Blast:
Prepositions of Place

Worksheet 14.2
Vocabulary Development:
Matching

Worksheet 14.3
Speaking and Listening:
Getting Around Town

Worksheet 14.4
Reading and Fluency

Worksheet 14.5
Daily Review

STEP 4: LANGUAGE BLAST *10 MINUTES*

(Teach/Guided Practice/Practice) Ask students how they show other people where to go or how to find things. Give examples of prepositions of place, while making visual demonstrations. For instance, you can place a book on a desk while saying: *the book is on the desk*. Move the book around (*in* the desk, *in front of* Juan, *behind* Sari, *beside* Tito). Distribute Worksheet 14.1 and allow students 5–10 minutes to complete it.

STEP 5: VOCABULARY DEVELOPMENT *10 MINUTES*

(Teach/Practice/Apply) Distribute Worksheet 14.2. Ask students if they know any of the words or recognize any of the pictures. Point to and carefully read each word in the list. Then show students how to complete the activity. Be sure to offer assistance as students complete Worksheet 14.2.

STEP 6: GRAMMAR AND CONVENTIONS *15 MINUTES*

(Guided Practice) Continue working with prepositions of place. Try this activity to get the students physically involved. Have students move anywhere in the classroom. They may stand alone, or with friends, in the front or in the back. Ask questions based on what you see: *Is Jose behind or in front of Kim?* When you get a correct response, turn your question into a statement: *Jose is in front of Kim.*

SPEAKING AND LISTENING

(Practice/Apply) To reinforce prepositions of place, distribute Worksheet 14.3 and allow students to work in pairs. Have students ask each other questions using words in the word bank to help them complete the place names on their maps. Allow about 7 minutes for this activity. Then correct the worksheet, reviewing each item as you go, before moving on to Worksheet 14.4.

STEP 7: READING AND FLUENCY *12 MINUTES*

(Apply/Review) Distribute a copy of Worksheet 14.4 to each student. You might have to explain riddles and give examples before students begin the activity. Check the activity in class or collect papers and correct them when the lesson is finished.

Teaching Tip
You may want to use simple demonstrations when introducing the vocabulary words. For example, use an eraser to demonstrate prepositions (on the table, under the table, in the desk, across the room, beside the board, to the left of the flag, and so on). Use magazine pictures or mime to suggest places, such as a restaurant, post office, bank, bus stop, shopping center.

Note: To allow for further review, Worksheet 14.5 may be assigned as homework.

Worksheet 14.5 Note
In this activity, encourage students to contribute to the discussion. Ask them to share knowledge of any words they recognize. This will help students become involved and gain a feeling of having a basic knowledge on which to build.

Worksheet 14.1: Language Blast

Prepositions of Place

in	on	at	over
under	behind	in front of	beside
to the left	to the right	across from	around

DIRECTIONS Look around the classroom. Find objects that are in different places. List the prepositions of place that you see in the classroom. Use the prepositions of place that are shown above.

1. The book is on the shelf _____.

2. _____.

3. _____.

4. _____.

5. _____.

Worksheet 14.2: Vocabulary Development

Matching

DIRECTIONS Look at the first column. These are names of different places. In the second column, there are things people do. Draw lines to match each place with the thing people do there.

1. bank

2. post office

3. movie theater

4. restaurant

5. museum

6. library

7. shopping center

8. supermarket

9. hospital

10. bus stop

A. mail a package

B. see a movie

C. see an art exhibit

D. take the bus

E. cash a check

F. get some milk

G. visit a sick friend

H. borrow a book

I. buy new clothes

J. have dinner

Worksheet 14.3: Speaking and Listening

Getting Around Town

DIRECTIONS Work with a partner. One partner should ask the first five questions. The other partner should ask the second five questions.

A. Ask your partner to help you find the places in the word bank below.

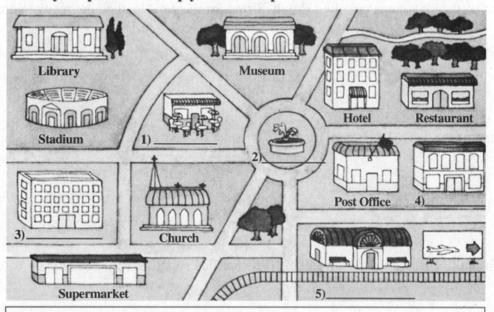

> **Where is the . . ?** bank, café, train station, hospital, bus stop

B. Ask your partner to help you find the places in the word bank below.

> **Where is the . . ?** supermarket, restaurant, library, post office, museum

Worksheet 14.4: Reading and Fluency

Reading for Understanding

DIRECTIONS Read each clue. Then guess the answer to the riddle.

1. Wait by the tracks for what is traveling slowly, listen for the whistle, then get ready to go.

Where are you? You are at a _____.

2. Here you mail out a letter, or come for a stamp, or send off a sweater or an old dusty lamp.

Where are you? You are at a _____.

3. Every shelf in this place is piled high full of treats, needed supplies, and tons of good eats.

Where are you? You are at a _____.

4. You come here to cheer and root for the team; to catch a fly ball would be just like a dream.

Where are you? You are at a _____.

5. Stop here to sleep if you are in a strange city; the view from your room is often quite pretty.

Where are you? You are at a _____.

Worksheet 14.5: Daily Review

DIRECTIONS Think of a place where you like to eat or shop. Pretend you are telling a friend how to meet you there. Answer these questions. Use at least five prepositions of place.

1. What street is this place on?

_____

_____

2. What is inside this place?

_____

_____

3. What is the place across from?

_____

_____

4. What is next to this place?

_____

_____

5. What is behind this place?

_____

_____

Lesson 15: Chores and Preparing for an Exam

STEP 1: WORD DRILL *2 MINUTES*

(Teach/Guided Practice) Greet the class, and then say: *I have chores to do. I have papers to correct. I have to clean the board.* Have the class repeat what you have said. After the class has repeated these words, say: *I need to clean the board now.* Again, ask students to repeat this sentence. Then say: *I am cleaning the board now.* Demonstrate this action by using an eraser to clean the chalkboard.

(Guided Practice) Point to individual students and have them repeat your words. Introduce a new vocabulary word in each sentence. Say: *I have chores to do. I have to make my bed. I have a test. I need to study.* As students repeat what you say, listen to their pronunciations. Make corrections as needed.

STEP 2: BUILD BACKGROUND *8 MINUTES*

(Teach/Guided Practice/Practice) Have students practice speaking about chores by following the short dialogue below. Write the dialogue on the board and read the first two lines aloud, using an expressive voice. Gesture for students to repeat as you read each line. Keep repeating until students are comfortable reciting the dialogue.

Let each student practice telling about chores, starting the dialogue from the beginning each time. After each student has had a turn to mention a chore from the lesson vocabulary, read the remaining four lines of dialogue. Repeat until students are comfortable pronouncing the words. Then say the first line (A) and ask the class to respond with the second line (B). When the class seems comfortable with the new vocabulary words, have students practice the dialogue with a partner. Have students take turns reading lines A and B. Walk around the room and monitor students' progress.

A: Do you have chores to do?

B: Yes, I have chores to do. I have to sweep the floor.

A: I have chores to do, too.

B: What chores do you have to do?

A: I have to make my bed. I need to study.

B: I need to study, too.

STEP 3: INDEPENDENT RECITATION *3 MINUTES*

(Apply) Give students time to memorize the opening dialogue of Step 2 and have volunteers recite it from memory in front of the class.

LESSON OBJECTIVES
Students will:

- practice proper pronunciation of vocabulary words and phrases
- use simple sentences to ask and answer questions about chores and exams
- produce simple vocabulary to communicate in an academic setting
- listen to, understand, and follow both written and oral instructions
- listen to and respond to peers as they describe their chores and exam preparations
- independently interact with peers

LESSON VOCABULARY
clean the room, sweep the floor, take out the trash, make the bed, dust the furniture, vacuum the carpet, study, read, review, practice an instrument, practice a sport

LESSON RESOURCES
Worksheet 15.1
Language Blast: Prepositions of Place

Worksheet 15.2
Vocabulary Development Matching

Worksheet 15.3
Speaking and Listening Present Continuous Verbs

Worksheet 15.4
Reading and Fluency

Worksheet 15.5
Daily Review

STEP 4: LANGUAGE BLAST *10 MINUTES*

(Teach/Guided Practice/Practice) Review prepositions of place by choosing a student volunteer and positioning him or her to demonstrate each of the following sentences. Say each sentence aloud, placing emphasis on the preposition.

_____ is *in* the room.

_____ is *on* the floor.

_____ is *behind* the desk.

_____ is *in front of* the trash can.

_____ is *beside* the teacher.

Ask students to name other prepositions of place. Examples include *at, over, under, to the left, to the right, across from,* and *around.* Point to a few students and ask them to use prepositions of place to describe objects in the classroom (*The chalkboard is under the clock.* or *The map is on the wall.*). Distribute Worksheet 15.1 and allow students 5–7 minutes to complete it.

STEP 5: VOCABULARY DEVELOPMENT *10 MINUTES*

(Teach/Practice/Apply) Distribute Worksheet 15.2. Begin by asking students to read the captions to see if they recognize any vocabulary words. Have students say the words aloud. Help them pronounce any difficult words. Ask students to work in pairs to complete the worksheet. Have them match pictures and captions. Monitor the students' interaction and correct pronunciation errors.

STEP 6: GRAMMAR AND CONVENTIONS *15 MINUTES*

(Guided Practice) Write on the board *I am, You are, He/she/it is, We are,* and *They are.* Explain that the present continuous form of a verb combines the words *am, is,* or *are* with the present participle: a verb that ends in *-ing.* Tell students that this form describes actions that are taking place right now. Demonstrate the different forms. Say: *I am reading a book.* Ask students to repeat this sentence. Say: *You are studying English.* Select a few students to stand in front of the class. Point to them and say: *They are reviewing new words.*

SPEAKING AND LISTENING

(Practice/Apply) Once students seem comfortable with the present continuous form, distribute Worksheet 15.3 and allow them 5–6 minutes to complete it in pairs. Check for correct pronunciation and correct any grammar errors.

STEP 7: READING AND FLUENCY *12 MINUTES*

(Apply/Review) Distribute Worksheet 15.4 to each student. If time allows, choose a few students to read aloud the first part of the worksheet. If not, students should read independently and answer the follow-up questions. Correct as a class, or collect pages and correct when the lesson is finished.

Teaching Tip During Step 4, encourage students to demonstrate place prepositions by using props or their own bodies. Ask volunteers to perform actions and have the rest of the class use words to describe those actions.

Optional Charades Game 10-15 minutes
Photocopy Game 6 on page 157. Cut out the verb phrases, fold them, and drop them in a bag. After students complete Worksheet 15.3, call on a volunteer to choose an activity from the bag and pantomime it for the class. Have students raise their hands when they know the answer. Choose a student and have that student use the present continuous to express the action in order to be considered correct. Then that student comes up and chooses something from the bag. The game continues until all slips of paper have been chosen.

Worksheet 15.4 Note
In this activity, students will encounter unfamiliar words. Guide students to infer the meanings of unfamiliar words to better understand the selection.

Note: To allow for further review, Worksheet 15.5 may be assigned as homework.

Worksheet 15.1: Language Blast

Prepositions of Place

DIRECTIONS Look at each picture. Read the sentence next to each picture.
Write the preposition of place that will best complete each sentence.

1. She is sweeping the floor _____ the kitchen.

.2 The trashcan is _____ the house.

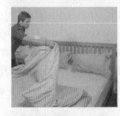

3. He is _____ the bed.

4. The boy is _____ the girl.

5. The girl is looking _____ the book.

6. The girl's guitar is _____ her lap.

Worksheet 15.2: Vocabulary Development

Matching

DIRECTIONS With a partner, read aloud the captions below the pictures. Then match each caption to the correct picture. Place the letter of the caption on the line next to the correct picture.

1. _____

2. _____

3. _____

4. _____

5. _____

6. _____

7. _____

8. _____

9. _____

10.  _____

A. make the bed

B. practice an instrument

C. take out the trash

D. dust the furniture

E. vacuum the carpet

F. practice a sport

G. study

H. read

I. clean the room

J. sweep the floor

Worksheet 15.3: Speaking and Listening

Present Continuous Verbs

DIRECTIONS Complete each sentence with the present continuous form of the verb phrase below. Then read each sentence aloud to a partner.

1. I _____.

   (clean the room)

2. You _____.

   (sweep the floor)

3. He _____.

   (take out the trash)

4. She _____.

   (make the bed)

5. They _____.

   (dust the furniture)

6. He _____.

   (vacuum the carpet)

7. I _____.

   (study for a test)

8. We _____.

   (read a book)

9. They _____.

   (practice a sport)

10. You _____.

   (play an instrument)

Worksheet 15.4: Reading and Fluency

Reading for Understanding

DIRECTIONS Read the following article.

How to Prepare for an Exam

When you study for an exam, there is a right way to study and a wrong way to study. If you study the right way, you will most likely do well. You need to begin studying many days before the day of the exam. This gives you time to ask questions if you do not understand something. Review your notes. Read parts of your textbook again. Study with a partner. Help each other understand difficult information. Make up a quiz for each other. Taking the quiz will help you practice for the test. Don't forget to take breaks when you study. Study for an hour. Then relax for ten minutes. This gives you time to remember the information you just learned. It also gives your brain a rest. Make flashcards to help you learn new words or remember new information. Get a good night's sleep before the exam. You do not want to fall asleep during the test! On the day of the exam, bring pens, pencils, and an eraser. Say to yourself, *I am ready. I will get a good grade on this test.* Then just do your best.

DIRECTIONS Read each sentence and tell whether it is true or false. Write *True* if the sentence is true. If the sentence is false, rewrite it to make it true.

1. You should start studying the night before the exam.

_____

2. Practice for an exam by making up quizzes with a study partner.

_____

3. Never take breaks when you are studying for an exam.

_____

4. Flashcards are not helpful for studying.

_____

5. You should get plenty of sleep the night before an exam.

_____

6. The most important thing to remember is to just do your best.

_____

Worksheet 15.5: Daily Review

My Chores

DIRECTIONS On the lines below, write a short paragraph about the chores you do each day. Be sure to answer ALL questions to help you plan your writing.

1. What chores do you do in the morning?
2. What chores do you do in the afternoon?
3. What chores do you do in the evening?
4. What is your least favorite chore?
5. Do you have any chores that you like doing?

_____

_____

_____

_____

_____

_____

_____

_____

_____

_____

_____

Lesson 16: Time

STEP 1: WORD DRILL *2 MINUTES*

(Teach/Guided Practice) Look at the clock on the wall. Ask students: *What time is it*? Then say, *It is (time) o'clock*. Ask students to repeat this phrase with you.

(Practice) After students have echoed as a class, write the following words on the board: *lunch, gym, home*. Explain to students that they usually go to these places or classes at a certain time. Ask the class: *When do you go to lunch*? Ask students if they know when their class goes to lunch. Have the class repeat the correct time: *We go to lunch at (time) o'clock*. Repeat this exercise by asking students to explain when they go to gym class and when they go home for the day.

STEP 2: UNDERSTANDING TIME, *8 MINUTES*

(Teach/Guided Practice) This is a continuation of Step 1 and can be used to show students how to explain when they do specific activities during the day. This can also help them explain events that have already taken place. Write these sentences on the board and read them aloud to the class:

I go to sleep at nine o'clock.

I get to school at eight o'clock.

I eat lunch at twelve o'clock.

Circle the word *at* in each of these sentences. Explain that *at* helps us understand when the events take place. Ask students to repeat the sentences on the board with you. Have a volunteer point out the times on the clock as you say them. This will help students connect the sentences on the board with the numbers on the clock.

STEP 3 : INDEPENDENT RECITATION, *3 MINUTES*

(Apply) Have students work in pairs to practice the following dialogue.

A: When do you wake up in the morning?

B: I wake up at (time) o'clock.
Students should take turns asking and answering the question. When they have finished, ask volunteers to tell their partners' answers. (Student's name) wakes up at (time) o'clock.

LESSON OBJECTIVES
Students will:

- learn and understand important words associated with time (morning, afternoon, evening, a.m., p.m.)
- learn how to form simple past-tense verbs
- understand how to use *at* when describing a specific time.
- work with partners to create dialogues that describe specific events
- listen to instructions and to peers' dialogue

LESSON VOCABULARY
talk, say, think, do, make, see, and practice prepositions of place (in, on, at)

LESSON RESOURCES
Worksheet 16.1
Language Blast: Time (with *at*)

Worksheet 16.2
Vocabulary Development: Answering A Reporter's Questions

Worksheet 16.3
Speaking and Listening: My Favorite Day

Worksheet 16.4
Reading and Fluency

Worksheet 16.5
Daily Review

Teaching Tip When teaching time, review the spellings of numbers one through twelve. Write each number and have students write the correct spelling next to each number.

Note: To allow for further review, Worksheet 16.5 may be assigned as homework.

STEP 4: TIME (WITH *AT*), *10 MINUTES*

(Teach/Guided Practice) Explain that the word *at* explains a specific time that an activity takes place. The word *at* is often used to explain things that we do on a regular basis. Use these sentences as examples:

I go to work at seven o'clock.

I walk the dog at four o'clock.

I eat dinner at six o'clock.

Introduce the ideas of A.M. and P.M. to the students. Draw two clocks on the board. Draw a moon over one and a sun over the other. Explain that twelve o'clock divides the day into morning hours (A.M.) and afternoon or evening hours (P.M). Show students when twelve o'clock is noon and when it is midnight. Have students express the sentences that follow using A.M. or P.M.:

I go to work at seven o'clock in the morning. (seven A.M.)

I walk the dog at four o'clock in the afternoon. (four P.M.)

I eat dinner at six o'clock in the evening. (six P.M.)

Then have students complete Worksheet 16.1 and review students' answers in class.

STEP 5 : VOCABULARY AND GRAMMAR IN SPEAKING, *10 MINUTES*

(Teach/Practice/Apply) Distribute a copy of Worksheet 16.2 to each student. Explain that reporters interview people. In an interview, the reporter asks questions to learn about another person's life and ideas. Give students 5 minutes to complete Worksheet 16.2. Then divide students into pairs. Tell students that they will perform a listening and speaking exercise with a partner. In this exercise, one student will pretend to be a reporter and the other will be a student. The report will ask the questions about the student's weekend and the student will answer. Encourage students to use vocabulary words, including prepositions of place, to give a detailed description of the weekend. After one student has played the part of the reporter, have students switch roles. Ask volunteers to read their interviews to the class.

Game 7
Optional Time Game: What Time Is It? *10-15 minutes*
Photocopy the Optional Time Game on page 158. Provide each student with a piece of paper. Cut out the paper clock and arms provided on page 158 and attach the arms with tack pin. Be sure that arms can move freely around the clock's face, but can also stay in place securely. Tell the students that you will be moving the clock's arms to show a specific time. When you ask: *What time is it?* students should write the correct time on their papers. Remind students to write out the time. Students with the correct answer will be awarded one point. The first student(s) to get five correct answers wins. Reward winner(s) with points or prizes.

Worksheet 16.3 Note
In this activity, some students may want to form irregular past-tense verbs that are not formed by adding *–d* or *–ed*. In this case, take the time to show the class how verbs ending in a consonant + y are formed (*try = tried*). Also explain that a consonant will sometimes need to be doubled before adding *–ed* (*trap = trapped*). Review common irregular past-tense verbs such as go/went; buy/bought; give/gave.

STEP 6: PAST TENSE REGULAR, *15 MINUTES*

(Guided Practice) Write the following dialogue on the board.

A: Think of your favorite day. What did you do on this day?

B: I baked cookies with my grandmother.
Circle the word *baked* in the second sentence. Explain that this is the regular past tense form of the verb *bake*. Show students that by adding the *d* to the end of *bake*, you formed the past tense of the verb. Many verbs can be changed to the past tense by adding *–d*. Write a few examples of these verbs on the board.
(*live* + *-d= lived*, *place* + *-d= placed*, *move* + *-d= moved*)
Explain that other words add *–ed* to form the past tense. These words do not have an *–e* at the end of the word.
(*talk* + *-ed= talked*, *jump* + *-ed= jumped*)
Have students explain their favorite days to each other before moving on to Worksheet 16.3.

(Practice/Apply)

Encourage students to explain their favorite days in much detail as possible, including when and where events took place. Then have students complete Worksheet 16.3. Correct it together and move on to Worksheet 16.4.

STEP 7 APPLICATION READING AND FLUENCY *12 MINUTES*

(Apply/Review) Distribute a copy of Worksheet 16.4 to each student. If time allows, choose a few students to read aloud the selection in the first part of the worksheet. If not, students should read independently and answer the follow-up questions. Correct papers in class or collect them and correct when the lesson is finished.

Worksheet 16.1: Language Blast

Time (with *at*)

DIRECTIONS Look at the time on each clock. Choose the answer that best matches each clock and tell what you do at that time.

1.
A. five o'clock   C. eleven fifty
B. six fifty   D. twelve o'clock

2.
A. eight o'clock   C. two thirty
B. nine o'clock   D. eleven o'clock

3.
A. two twenty   C. four o'clock
B. three twenty   D. five o'clock

4.
A. two thirty   C. eleven o'clock
B. seven o'clock   D. twelve thirty

5.
A. three fifty five   C. five o'clock
B. four o'clock   D. six fifty five

6.
A. five o'clock   C. seven fifteen
B. six o'clock   D. eight fifteen

7.
A. six o'clock   C. ten o'clock
B. seven forty five   D. nine o'clock

8.
A. twelve o'clock   C. two o'clock
B. one o'clock   D. three o'clock

Worksheet 16.2: Vocabulary Development

Answer a Reporter's Questions

DIRECTIONS Pretend you are talking to a reporter. The reporter wants to know what you did this weekend. Answer the reporter's questions using complete sentences. When you answer, you may pretend that you have just returned from a faraway place. Give as much description about the time and place as possible.

1. What did you do this weekend? _____

_____

2. What time did this happen? _____

_____

3. Where did this happen? _____

_____

4. Who was with you?_____

_____

5. What was he/she doing? _____

_____

6. What time did you arrive? _____

_____

7. What did you see? _____

_____

8. Did you have a good time? _____

_____

Worksheet 16.3: Speaking and Listening

My Favorite Day

DIRECTIONS Think about a great day from your past. What made this day special? Where did you go? What did you do? Who was with you? Describe the day you remember on the lines below, then read it aloud to the class.

_____

_____

_____

_____

_____

_____

_____

_____

_____

_____

_____

_____

_____

_____

Worksheet 16.4: Reading and Fluency

Reading for Understanding

DIRECTIONS Read the announcement below.

Spring Fair

Come to the Spring Fair on Saturday, March 1st - 11:00 A.M. to 9:00 P.M.
Tickets go on sale February 18th .
Student tickets cost $4.00. Parent tickets cost $5.00.

12:00 P.M. Drama Club performance
2:00 P.M. Three-legged race on the soccer field
5:00-7:00 P.M. Band plays near the flagpole
6:00 P.M. Bingo begins under the tent
8:00 P.M. Fireworks on the football field

Remember to get your tickets early!
All money collected will be donated to Children's Hospital.

DIRECTIONS Read each question carefully. Write the correct answer in the space provided in a complete sentence.

1. What day is the Spring Fair? _____.

2. When do tickets go on sale for the fair? _____.

3. How much do student tickets cost? _____.

4. At what time will the three-legged race start? _____.

5. Where will the band be playing? _____.

6. When does Bingo start? _____.

7. Where will the fireworks be?_____.

Worksheet 16.5: Daily Review

Time

DIRECTIONS Look at each clock. Choose the correct time. Then write a sentence about what you were doing at this time yesterday. Write your answers in complete sentences.

1.

   A. seven fifteen   B. eight o'clock

   C. five o'clock   D. six thirty

   _____

2.

   A. eight o'clock   B. eleven thirty

   C. ten o'clock   D. two thirty

   _____.

3.

   A. nine o'clock   B. ten fifteen

   C. eleven o'clock   D. twelve o'clock

   _____.

4.

   A. twelve thirty   B. one o'clock

   C. two o'clock   D. three o'clock

   _____.

5.

   A. two o'clock   B. three fifty five

   C. four fifty five   D. five o'clock

   _____.

Lesson 17: Don't Be Late!

STEP 1: WORD DRILL *2 MINUTES*
(Teach/Guided Practice) Briefly review time words and past tense verbs from Lesson 16. Then teach the use of the word *not* to show a negative action. Point out how the verb changes when the word *not* is used. Write these sentences on the board:

I talked to my brother
I did not talk to my brother.

Expand these sentences to include a review of prepositions of place from Lesson 16 (*I did not talk to my brother on the phone. I talked to my brother at the park.*).

Next, introduce the concept of being late. Use the example of being late to class. Ask: *What happens when you are late to class?* Students' answers should reflect the idea that being late leads to getting into trouble. Point out that people make excuses when they think they are late to avoid getting into trouble.

STEP 2: BUILD BACKGROUND *8 MINUTES*
(Teach/Guided Practice/Practice) Have students imagine being late for school. Ask: *Why are you late?* Students should generate a list of excuses for being late, using regular past tense verbs. Chose a few reasons and use them to create a dialogue on the board.

A: You are late.

B: You are late, too.

A: Why are you late?

B: I lost my homework. Why are you late?

A: I missed the school bus.

Read the dialogue aloud for students and ask them to repeat after you.

STEP 3: INDEPENDENT RECITATION *3 MINUTES*
(Apply) Have students practice the dialogue with partners. Students may add to the dialogue by coming up with additional excuses for being late. Monitor student interactions to ensure that students are using correct pronunciation and past tense forms. Ask a few pairs of students to perform their dialogues in front of the class.

LESSON OBJECTIVES
Students will:

- respond to questions about being late for an event, using regular and irregular past tense verbs
- learn new verbs and use them to describe events that took place in the past
- speak in complete sentences to make excuses
- use declarative sentences to describe themselves
- listen to and verbally interact with peers
- follow oral and written directions

LESSON VOCABULARY
to make an excuse, talk, say, think, do, make, practice, past tense of *to be*, *to have*, *have to*, and *need to*

LESSON RESOURCES
Worksheet 17.1
Language Blast: Trouble

Worksheet 17.2
Vocabulary Development:
Had to and *needed to*

Worksheet 17.3
Speaking and Listening:
Making Excuses

Worksheet 17.4
Reading and Fluency

Worksheet 17.5
Daily Review

Teaching Tip Consider using flashcards to help students remember verbs. On one side, print the present tense. On the back side, print the past tense. Include both regular and irregular verbs for students to review from time to time.

STEP 4: LANGUAGE BLAST *10 MINUTES*

(Teach/Guided Practice/Practice) Have nine students stand at the front of the room. Have each one represent a pronoun *(I, you, he, she, it, we, you,* and *they)*. Then write *to be* on the board. Tell students that some verbs have irregular conjugations. Tell them that the *I* form of *to be* is not *I be*. Point to yourself and say: *I am,* and write it on the board under the infinitive form of the verb. Have the student representing *I* repeat after you: *I am.* Then ask the entire class to repeat: *I am.* Follow this pattern for each form of the conjugated verb. Then repeat this pattern with the past tense form of *to be,* beginning with *I was.* Continue the activity with the irregular verbs *to say* and *to think.* First review present tense conjugations of the verbs. Then provide students with the conjugations in the past tense as well. Distribute Worksheet 17.1. Go over the verbs in the word bank and allow pairs or small groups 5–10 minutes to complete the worksheet orally.

STEP 5: VOCABULARY DEVELOPMENT *10 MINUTES*

(Teach/Practice/Apply) Review the use of *have to* and *need to* from Lesson 15 and teach their past tense forms. Make the distinction by first using the present tense form: *Today, I have to go to the library.* Then introduce the past tense: *Yesterday, I had to go to the bank.* Distribute Worksheet 17.2 and allow students 5 minutes to complete it.

STEP 6: GRAMMAR AND CONVENTIONS *15 MINUTES*

(Guided Practice) Have students share some of their sentences from Worksheet 17.2. Use these sentences to facilitate a discussion about making excuses. Write one of the students' situations on the board. (*I talked in class.*) Ask the student: *Why did you talk in class?* The student should respond: *I talked in class because I needed to ask a question.* Point to the use of *because* when making an excuse.

(PRACTICE/APPLY)

Distribute Worksheet 17.3 and preteach any new words on the sheet (absent, soccer). Then ask students to complete the worksheet. Students can then walk around the room and ask other students a question from the worksheet. Monitor responses and correct pronunciation if necessary.

STEP 7: READING AND FLUENCY *12 MINUTES*

(Apply/Review) Distribute Worksheet 17.4. Ask students if they have *curfews.* Explain the concept of a curfew. Then students should practice making excuses for missing a curfew. Students should ask each other: *Why were you late?* and then generate excuses for missing their curfew. Preteach new words in the story on Worksheet 17.4 and have students complete it in class.

Worksheet 17.2 Note
You might consider preparing handouts of conjugation charts for students to keep in their notebooks. When you have a few spare minutes, direct students' attention to the charts and ask questions or have students make up sentences using specific verbs.

Note: To allow for further review, Worksheet 17.5 may be assigned as homework.

Worksheet 17.1: Language Blast

Trouble

DIRECTIONS Use the words in word bank to tell about a time you got in trouble. Be sure to use the past tense in your sentences.

Word Bank

talk	say	think
do	make	practice

1. I once got in trouble because I _____

_____

2. I once got in trouble because I _____

_____

3. I once got in trouble because I _____

_____

4. I once got in trouble because I _____

_____

5. I once got in trouble because I _____

_____

Worksheet 17.2: Vocabulary Development

Had to and *Needed to*

DIRECTIONS Read each phrase. Decide if it describes an action in the present or the past. Then circle the correct verb form and complete the sentence.

1. Yesterday, I (have to / had to)

_____

2. Before we eat lunch today, I (need to / needed to)

_____

3. Right now, I (have to / had to)

_____

4. Last year, I (have to / had to)

_____

5. When I was a child, I (need to / needed to)

_____

6. Before tomorrow, I (need to / needed to)

_____

7. Every day when I wake up, I (have to / had to)

_____

8. Sometimes after class I (need to / needed to)

_____

9. A month ago, I (have to / had to)

_____

10. At ten o'clock last night, I (have to / had to)

_____

Worksheet 17.3: Speaking and Listening

Making Excuses

DIRECTIONS Answer each question in a complete sentence. Use *had to* or *needed to*.

1. Why didn't you study for the test? _____

_____

2. Why did you make a mess? _____

_____

3. Why were you late for soccer practice? _____

_____

4. Why were you absent from school? _____

_____

5. Why did you forget your lunch? _____

_____

6. Why were you up so late last night? _____

_____

7. Why didn't you do your homework? _____

_____

8. Why didn't you walk your dog? _____

_____

Worksheet 17.4: Reading and Fluency

Reading for Understanding

DIRECTIONS Read Chin's story. Then answer each question with a complete sentence, using the phrase *had to* or *needed to*.

Why Were You Late?

I was at the library with Kim. We were on our way home when it started to rain. We did not have an umbrella. So we had to wait in a doorway until the rain stopped. Then we decided to take a bus. We went to the bus stop. Kim got hungry waiting. I went to the store to buy her an apple.

While I was gone, I missed the bus. That meant we had to walk home. I needed to call and tell you I would be late. Kim and I walked around looking for a phone. We found a puppy that seemed lost. Kim said we had to find its owner. Finally, the owner came. She wanted to give us a reward. She bought us ice cream. Then I had to walk Kim home. Kim loaned me a bike so I could get home quickly. The bike got a flat tire and I brought it back. I had to walk anyway. This is why I am late.

1. Why did Chin and Kim stand in a doorway?

_____

_____

2. Why did Chin miss the bus?

_____

_____

3. Why did Chin and Kim look for a phone?

_____

_____

4. Why did Chin and Kim stop looking for a phone?

_____

_____

5. What happened right after Chin and Kim had ice cream?

_____

_____

Worksheet 17.5: Daily Review

Following the Rules

DIRECTIONS What are the rules in your house? Write a house rule on each *Rule* line. Make up a pretend excuse for not following the rule. Write it on the *Excuse* line.

1. Rule:

_____

Excuse:

_____

2. Rule:

_____

Excuse:

_____

3. Rule:

_____

Excuse:

_____

4. Rule:

_____

Excuse:

_____

5. Rule:

_____

Excuse:

_____

Lesson 18: Food and Drink

STEP 1: WORD DRILL 2 MINUTES

(Teach/Guided Practice) Ask students: *What do you like to eat?* Have students share names of favorite dishes that they eat at home. Ask students to tell the class what foods or ingredients are in those dishes.

(Guided Practice) Then ask students: *Who is hungry?* Instruct students who raise their hands to point to themselves and say: *I am hungry.* Instruct students who do not raise their hands to point to the other students and say: *He is hungry* or *She is hungry.* Use this exercise as an introduction to the irregular verb *to be.*

STEP 2: BUILD BACKGROUND 8 MINUTES

(Teach/Guided Practice/Practice)

Draw two conjugation charts on the board. Leave enough space to draw another chart next to each later in the lesson. Write *to be* above one chart and *to have* above the other. Then conjugate the present tense of each verb with students, prompting students to provide answers when they know which form of the verb belongs in the chart

STEP 3: INDEPENDENT RECITATION 3 MINUTES

(Apply) Ask students to discuss what they brought to school for lunch. Students should tell others in the classroom: *I have a sandwich* or *I have salad.* Then have students tell what another student has for lunch: *She has a sandwich* or *He has pasta.* Encourage students to use words to describe the foods (meat, vegetables, milk).

STEP 4: LANGUAGE BLAST 10 MINUTES

(Teach/Guided Practice/Practice) Draw the additional conjugation charts on the board. Above the original charts, write *Present.* Above the new charts, write *Past.* Explain to students that irregular verbs have irregular conjugations in the past tense as well. Conjugate the verbs *to be* and *to have* in the past tense, again seeking student input as you complete each chart. Say each word as you write it, and have students repeat each word after you. Pass out Worksheet 18.1. Then allow students 5–7 minutes to complete it.

STEP 5: VOCABULARY DEVELOPMENT 10 MINUTES

(Teach/Practice/Apply) Distribute a copy of Worksheet 18.2 to each student and ask if they can name a food or drink on the worksheet. Point to each picture and say the name of each food or drink. Have students repeat after you. Then discuss the phrases *I like* and *I do not like.* Ask students to describe foods that they do and not like. Have students explain why using the word *because.* As each student responds, write the explanatory phrases on the board (*tastes good, tastes bad, smells good, smells bad*). Assist students in using descriptive words. Then have students complete Worksheet 18.2.

LESSON OBJECTIVES
Students will:

- respond to basic questions using gestures and one-word answers
- learn and use new vocabulary related to food and drink
- use past and present irregular forms of the verbs *to be* and *to have*
- speak in complete sentences to describe food and drink
- use declarative sentences to describe likes and dislikes
- listen to and follow instructions
- listen to and interact with peers through dialogue

LESSON VOCABULARY
vegetables (carrot, broccoli, potato, tomato, pepper, lettuce, cucumber, onion), fruit (apple, pear, orange, watermelon, kiwi, cantaloupe, grape, blueberry, strawberry), chicken, fish, beef, ham, cheese, rice, pasta, sandwich, bread, soup, water, juice, soda, coffee, tea

LESSON RESOURCES
Worksheet 18.1
Language Blast:
Irregular Verbs

Worksheet 18.2
Vocabulary Development:
I Like/I Do Not Like

Worksheet 18.3
Listening and Speaking:
Classroom Cooking

Worksheet 18.4
Reading and Fluency

Worksheet 18.5
Daily Review

STEP 6: GRAMMAR AND CONVENTIONS *15 MINUTES*

(Guided Practice) Preteach food names (sandwich, carrot, chicken, bread, juice), modeling each term as you say it. Encourage students to mimic your phrases such as: *I like baked potatoes* while modeling eating baked potatoes.

SPEAKING AND LISTENING

(Practice/Apply) Pass out Worksheet 18.3 and model how to complete an item on the worksheet using a vocabulary word that does not appear on the worksheet. Students should use the new terms to complete Worksheet 18.3 with partners. Tell students that as they complete the worksheet, they should say the sentence aloud: *I am frying chicken* or *I am peeling the orange*. Partners should respond with the appropriate form of the irregular verb *to be*: *You are frying chicken* or *You are peeling the orange*.

STEP 7: READING AND FLUENCY *12 MINUTES*

(Apply/Review) Present students with Worksheet 18.4. Show students the recipe on this worksheet, and preteach any new words (cup, teaspoon, ingredients). Then have students complete the worksheet in class. Correct in class or collect papers and correct when the lesson is finished. Before the end of the lesson, preteach vocabulary from Worksheet 18.5.

Teaching Tip
When teaching fruits and vegetables, be sure to explain to students how some of the terms are related. Explain that broccoli and carrots are types of *vegetables*, and that apples and oranges are *fruits*. You might also introduce *sandwich* as being made of bread, ham, cheese, lettuce, and tomato. Illustrate this point by drawing pictures on the board or by pointing at the pictures on the worksheet. Encourage students to make up sandwiches or meals using the vocabulary words.

Worksheet 18.4 Note
In this activity, students will encounter unfamiliar words. Teachers may wish to preteach these words with examples (a can of beans, a can of corn, a measuring cup, a teaspoon) to help students connect with the activity.

Note: To allow for further review, Worksheet 18.5 may be assigned as homework.

Worksheet 18.1: Language Blast

Irregular Verbs in the Past Tense

DIRECTIONS Look at each pronoun on the left and draw a line to its
matching verb on the right. Some verbs may go with more than one pronoun.

Pronouns	**"To Be"**
I	
you	was
he / she / it	
we	were
you	
they	

Pronouns	**"To Have"**
I	
you	had
he / she / it	
we	
you	has
they	

Worksheet 18.2: Vocabulary Development

I Like / I Do Not Like

DIRECTIONS Look at each picture. Write the word for the food or drink in each picture.

1. _____

2. _____

3. _____

4. _____

5. _____

6. _____

7. _____

8. _____

9. _____

10. _____

11. _____

12. _____

Foods I Like

1. I like _____ because _____.

2. I like _____ because._____.

3. I like _____ because._____.

Foods I Do Not Like

4. I do not like _____ because _____.

5. I do not like _____ because _____.

6. I do not like _____ because _____.

Worksheet 18.3: Speaking and Listening

Classroom Cooking

DIRECTIONS Look at each picture. Ask your partner to write the name of the food that is shown. Write a sentence that tells how you like to eat each food. Then act out how you like to eat this food or drink.

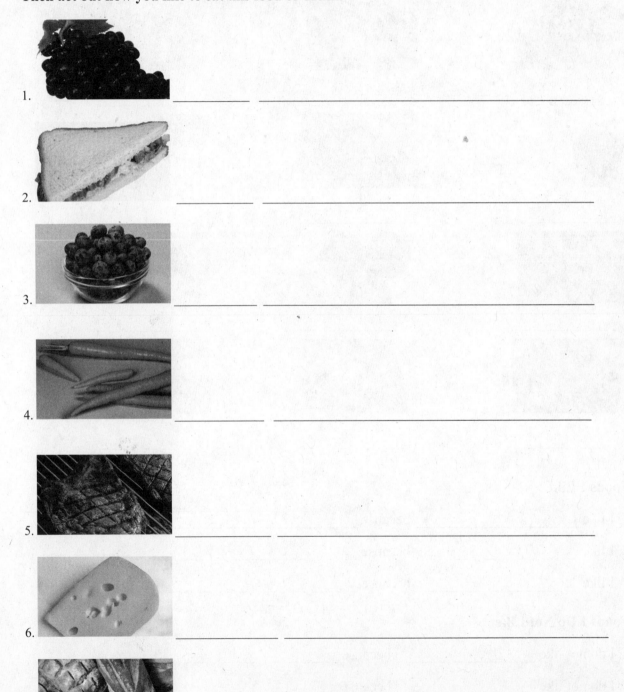

1. _____ _____

2. _____ _____

3. _____ _____

4. _____ _____

5. _____ _____

6. _____ _____

7. _____ _____

Worksheet 18.4: Reading and Fluency

Reading for Understanding

DIRECTIONS Read the recipe and the directions.

Stuffed Peppers

Ingredients:

3 peppers (red, green, or yellow)   1 15oz. can black beans, drained

1 cup corn   1 cup cooked rice

½ cup onions, chopped   2 oz. cheese, grated

¼ cup water   1 teaspoon black pepper

1 pinch chili powder   butter

You will need:

a glass pan   a pot (to cook the rice)

a knife   a measuring cup

a measuring spoon   a mixing bowl

a large spoon

Directions:

1. First, heat the oven to 350°F.

2. Then spread butter in a glass pan so the food does not stick to the pan.

3. Cook rice according to the directions on the package.

4. While rice is cooking, cut the peppers in half. Then cut out the seeds from the peppers.

5. Chop the onions into very small pieces.

6. Drain the beans and corn. Then mix all ingredients but the peppers, cheese, and water in a mixing bowl.

7. Place the pepper halves in the dish. Spoon the mixture onto the peppers.

8. Pour water into the bottom of the dish and cover with aluminum foil.

9. Bake for 30 minutes. While peppers are cooking, grate cheese. When peppers are done, sprinkle with grated cheese while still hot.

DIRECTIONS Circle *true* or *false* next to each sentence.

1. I chopped the onions before I mixed the ingredients.   True   False

2. I cooked the peppers before I sprinkled the cheese.   True   False

3. I cut the peppers after I spooned the mixture onto them.   True   False

4. I cooked the rice before I baked the peppers.   True   False

5. I drained the beans and corn before I mixed them.   True   False

Name _____ Class _____ Date _____

Worksheet 18.5: Daily Review

Nouns and Verbs

DIRECTIONS Fill in the missing verb forms in each chart.

To Be		
Pronoun	Present Tense Verb	Past Tense Verb
I	am	
you	are	
he/she/it		was
we	are	were
you	are	were
they		were

To Have		
Pronoun	Present Tense Verb	Past Tense Verb
I		had
you	have	had
he/she/it		had
we	have	
you	have	had
they		had

DIRECTIONS Use the information provided below to complete each sentence. The first one is done for you.

1. We + *to be* (past tense) + cut +   =
We were cutting lettuce.

2. I + *to have* (past tense) + a +   and
+ for lunch = _____

3. They + *to be* (present tense) + bake +   =
_____

4. You + *to have* (past tense) +   + for dinner =
_____

5. She + *to be* (present tense) + wash +   =
_____

Lesson 19: What Happened Last Weekend?

STEP 1: WORD DRILL *2 MINUTES*
(Teach/Guided Practice) Ask the class to contribute examples of verbs they have learned. Explain to them that verbs *go* and *get* are in the present tense. They are happening right now. Tell the class that past tense verbs describe things that have already happened.

(Guided Practice) After students understand the distinction between present and past tense verbs, ask for examples. Ask students to use verbs that tell about things that have already happened.

STEP 2: BUILD BACKGROUND *8 MINUTES*
(Teach/Guided Practice/Practice) This is a continuation of Step 1 and introduces the topic of irregular past-tense verbs. Draw a two-column chart on the board. Write examples of present tense verbs. Then write the past tenses of those words. Show the difference in tenses using these sentence frames:

A: Now I _____ in class.

B: Yesterday I _____ in class.

Use words such as *answer* and *answered* to show regular past tense. Use words such as *speak* and *spoke* to show irregular past tense.

STEP 3: INDEPENDENT RECITATION *3 MINUTES*
(Apply) Ask students to choose one irregular past tense verb and use it in a sentence. Be sure the sentence refers to something in the past and that the student uses the verb correctly. Ask each student to read the sentence aloud, and to then listen carefully to his or her peers as they read their sentences.

STEP 4: LANGUAGE BLAST *10 MINUTES*
(Teach/Guided Practice/Practice) Explain to students that irregular past tense verbs can be tricky because they change their spelling rather than just add *–d* or *–ed* to base words. Examples of present and past tense words that are completely different include: buy/bought; give/gave; think/thought. Assure students that, with practice, they will learn which verbs are correct and incorrect. Distribute Worksheet 19.1 and allow students 5–10 minutes to complete it.

STEP 5: VOCABULARY DEVELOPMENT *10 MINUTES*
(Teach/Practice/Apply) Distribute Worksheet 19.2.Explain that verbs change depending on when an action took place. You may do the same thing today as you did yesterday, but you would have to use a different verb to describe the action. Help students master this topic by taking them through the worksheet step by step. Have students read aloud the sentences and vocabulary words. Then have them identify whether the sentences and verbs are present or past tense.

LESSON OBJECTIVES
Students will:

- use phrases and short sentences in social settings
- recognize simple phrases about plans and actions
- use simple vocabulary to convey basic needs and ideas
- use comparatives and superlatives to identify ideas and actions
- listen to instructions and to peers' dialogue

LESSON VOCABULARY
begin, become, bring, buy, eat, drink, fall, feel, forget, fly, get, give, go, hear, know, meet, make, pay, read, run, send, say, see, take, teach, think, throw, understand, win, write

LESSON RESOURCES
Worksheet 19.1
Language Blast:
Irregular past tense verbs

Worksheet 19.2
Vocabulary Development:
Today and Yesterday

Worksheet 19.3
Speaking and Listening:
On the Weekend…

Worksheet 19.4
Reading and Fluency

Worksheet 19.5
Daily Review

Teaching Tip If students have difficulty distinguishing between present and past tenses, suggest that they use a sentence frame for the past: *Yesterday I ____ at the park.*

Note: To allow for further review, Worksheet 19.5 may be assigned as homework.

STEP 6: GRAMMAR AND CONVENTIONS *15 MINUTES*

(Guided Practice) Show the class a photo of yourself as a child or use a generic child picture, labeled as *a child*. Hold up the picture and use present and past verbs to talk about your childhood and your present life. For example, you can say: *When I was a child, I had a stuffed teddy bear*. and *Today I have a car*. Ask students to talk about themselves by describing their childhoods and the present.

SPEAKING AND LISTENING

(Practice/Apply) Give students practice with new vocabulary and irregular past-tense verbs by assigning Worksheet 19.3. This worksheet challenges students to write details about last weekend. Remind students that last weekend is the past and requires past tense verbs.

STEP 7: READING AND FLUENCY *12 MINUTES*

(Apply/Review) Distribute a copy of Worksheet 19.4 to each student. Help prepare students for the reading exercise by having a few students share what they wrote in the previous exercise Write their sentences on the board and have the class recite them with you.

Worksheet 19.1: Language Blast

Irregular Past Tense Verbs

DIRECTIONS Look at this chart of irregular past tense verbs. Then complete each sentence below with the correct verb tense.

Present Tense	Past Tense
bring	brought
buy	bought
eat	ate
drink	drank
get	got
go	went
meet	met
read	read
see	saw
take	took

1. On cold days I _____ (to drink) hot tea.

2. We _____ (to take) the books to the library yesterday.

3. From my window I _____ (to see) pretty birds.

4. Mateo and Leika _____ (to buy) new hats at the fair last month.

5. My friends _____ (to go) to see a new movie last weekend.

6. We _____ (to meet) my cousins at the mall and had fun.

7. At school we _____ (to read) many stories.

8. Sometimes I _____ (to get) to have my favorite meal.

Worksheet 19.2: Vocabulary Development

Today and Yesterday

DIRECTIONS Read each sentence pair. The first sentence tells what happens today. The second sentence tells the same thing as if it happened yesterday. Complete each sentence with the irregular past tense verb form. The first is done for you.

1. A. Present tense: We go to the biggest lake in the state.

   B. Past tense: We __went__ to the biggest lake in the state.

2. A. Present tense: I see pretty clouds in the sky.

   B. Past tense: I _____ pretty clouds in the sky.

3. A. Present tense: Rosa and Linda eat tortillas.

   B. Past tense: Rosa and Linda _____ tortillas.

4. A. Present tense: The dog brings me the newspaper.

   B. Past tense: The dog _____ me the newspaper.

5. A. Present tense: I take a day off because I am sick.

   B. Past tense: I _____ a day off because I was sick.

6. A. Present tense: Some people get milk with their lunch.

   B. Past tense: Some people _____ milk with their lunch.

7. A. Present tense: Jose falls on the ice.

   B. Past tense: Jose _____ on the ice.

Worksheet 19.3: Speaking and Listening

On the Weekend...

DIRECTIONS Use your new vocabulary words to write sentences about things you did last weekend. You can make up a pretend story about the weekend if you like. Use at least five vocabulary words from the word bank. Then tell the class about your weekend.

Word Bank

become	bring	buy	eat	drink
feel	get	give	go	hear
meet	read	say	see	take

What did you do last weekend?

Last weekend I ...

_____

_____

_____

_____

_____

_____

_____

_____

Share your answers with the class!

Worksheet 19.4: Reading and Fluency

Irregular Past Tense Verbs

DIRECTIONS Read this short story.

A Great Pet

Carlos wanted a pet. His mother said they could not get a dog. Dogs make too much noise. Carlos knew he could not get a cat either. Cat hair made people sneeze. Carlos did not think it would be fun to have a fish. "How much fun is a fish that swims in a bowl all day?" he wondered.

On Saturday, Carlos visited his Uncle Alex. Carlos told Uncle Alex that he wanted a pet. Uncle Alex said he had a good idea. "I know what animal is just right for you," said Uncle Alex. "It is quieter than a dog. It does not have fur that makes people sneeze. It is a lot of fun!"

Uncle Alex left and came back with a little clear box. Inside the box was a hamster. The hamster looked like a fuzzy mouse. The hamster ran around happily. It was fun to watch.

"That looks like a great pet," said Carlos. "Where can I get one?"

DIRECTIONS Answer these questions about the story. Write your answers in complete sentences. Use irregular past tense verbs in your answers.

1. Why didn't Carlos's mother want a dog?

_____

2. Why didn't Carlos want a fish?

_____

3. What kind of pet did Uncle Alex have?

_____

4. What did Uncle Alex think about hamsters?

_____

5. What did Carlos want to know at the end of the story?

_____

_____

Worksheet 19.5: Daily Review

Irregular Past Tense Verbs

DIRECTIONS Read each sentence. Each sentence tells about the past. If the
sentence is correct, circle the word *Correct*. If the sentence is not correct,
circle *Incorrect* and rewrite the sentence correctly on the line.

1. Last year my parents took me to a nice restaurant for my birthday.

   Correct   Incorrect

   _____

2. In 1999, my teacher first meet her husband.

   Correct   Incorrect

   _____

3. Yesterday I see my friends at the park.

   Correct   Incorrect

   _____

4. When I was a baby, I ate baby food.

   Correct   Incorrect

   _____

5. Last Tuesday, Diego bought a pair of running shoes.

   Correct   Incorrect

   _____

6. A few days ago, I bring the wrong book to school.

   Correct   Incorrect

   _____

Lesson 20: Place Settings/At A Party

STEP 1: WORD DRILL *2 MINUTES*
(Teach/Guided Practice) Bring in pictures of common utensils and dishes you would find at a dinner party. These would include a fork, knife, spoon, cup, bowl, plate, and glass. As you point to each picture, say the name of the object. Ask students to repeat each of these words with you.

(Guided Practice) Write the following questions on the board. Model the first sentence for students before asking volunteers for answers to the questions that follow.

1. I drink water out of a _____. (Explain that the *cup* or *glass* would both be acceptable answers.)

2. I eat soup using a _____.

3. I put my cereal in a _____.

4. I wipe my hands with a _____.

STEP 2: BUILD BACKGROUND *8 MINUTES*
(Teach/Guided Practice/Practice) This is a continuation of Step 1 and helps students practice irregular past tense verbs. Write the following dialogue on the board:

A: What did you eat at the dinner party?

B: I ate (chicken and vegetables).

Circle the word *ate*. Remind students that this is the past tense of the verb *eat*. Have volunteers name other irregular past tense verbs that they learned in Lesson 19. Ask students to repeat the sentences on the board with you, substituting their favorite foods in the sentence.

STEP 3: INDEPENDENT RECITATION *3 MINUTES*
(Apply) Pair students. Have students ask each other the following questions. Students should respond using the correct past tense of the verb in their answers.

1. What did you bring to the dinner party?

2. Who did you meet at the party?

3. What did you drink at the party?

4. What did you eat at the party?

Students should take turns asking and answering the questions. When they have finished, ask volunteers to recite their dialogues to the class.

LESSON OBJECTIVES
Students will:
- learn words associated with place settings and parties
- review forming past tense irregular verbs
- understand how modals are used with present tense verbs
- work together to answer questions
- pay close attention to instructions and offer feedback to their peers

LESSON VOCABULARY
plate, cup, napkin, spoon, fork, knife, bowl, glass; review of irregular past tense verbs and helping verbs.

LESSON RESOURCES
Worksheet 20.1
Language Blast:
Time (with *at*)

Worksheet 20.2
Vocabulary Development:
How do I use my utensils?

Worksheet 20.3
Speaking and Listening:
More past tense irregular verbs

Worksheet 20.4
Reading and Fluency

Worksheet 20.5
Daily Review

Teaching Tip Students might need to spend extra time so that they understand helping verbs, such as *could, might, ought to, shall,* and so on. Explain that these words indicate time and voice.

STEP 4: LANGUAGE BLAST *10 MINUTES*

(Teach/Guided Practice/Practice) Review past tense irregular verbs that students learned in Lesson 19. Write the following sentences on the board. Ask student volunteers to come to the board and circle the correct form of the verb for each sentence:

1. Sonia (bringed/brought) iced tea to the party.

2. Sal (made/maked) apple pie for the party.

3. Dolores (bought/buyed) flowers for the party's host.

Ask students to describe other actions that would be appropriate at a dinner party. Remind students to use the past tense. Ask them to identify whether the verb in their sentence is regular or irregular. When students have a good grasp of these sentences, have them complete Worksheet 20.1 on their own.

STEP 5: VOCABULARY DEVELOPMENT *10 MINUTES*

(Teach/Practice/Apply) Give each student a piece of paper. Instruct them to draw a place setting and label each of the items. Draw a large place setting on the board. Ask students to name each of the items they see. Ask students to compare and contrast their place settings to the one on the board. Ask: *Is anything missing from their place settings? Can students think of other utensils that might be at a dinner party (serving spoons, butter knives)?* Review food words and prepositions from Lesson 18 with students. Encourage students to name utensils that go with each food. This will help prepare them for Worksheet 20.2. Give students time to complete the worksheet on their own. When they have finished, go over the answers together. Ask volunteers to recite some of their answers aloud to the class.

STEP 6: GRAMMAR AND CONVENTIONS *15 MINUTES*

(Guided Practice) Write the following verbs and their irregular past tense forms on the board:

begin (began)	fall (fell)
forget (forgot)	fly (flew)
know (knew)	make (made)
pay (paid)	run (ran)
send (sent)	teach (taught)
think (thought)	throw (threw)
win (won)	write (wrote)
understand (understood)	

Next, write the following on the board:
I run to the store today. I ran to the store yesterday.

Game 8
Optional Game:
Party Matching Game:
Vocabulary
10-15 minutes

Photocopy Party Matching Game on page 159. Tell students to cut out the words and pictures. After they have cut out all of the squares, have students match the words to the correct pictures. The first student who successfully completes the match, wins. Continue playing until you have three winners. Provide points or prizes for winner(s).

Worksheet 20.2 Note
Have students look over the vocabulary from lesson 19 before they start. This will give them a jump on the worksheet.

Note: To allow for further review, Worksheet 20.5 may be assigned as homework.

Circle the words *run* and *ran*. Explain that *ran* is the irregular past tense form of the verb *run*. Ask students to use one of the verbs on the board in a present tense sentence and then in a past tense sentence. Students may write the words *today* and *yesterday* in their sentences to help them use the correct tense of the verb.

SPEAKING AND LISTENING

(Practice/Apply) After students have written their own sentences, have them to begin work on Worksheet 20.3. Correct the worksheet together and answer any questions students have about forming the irregular past tense.

STEP 7: READING AND FLUENCY *12 MINUTES*

(Apply/Review) Introduce the following words: *can, could, may, might, must, ought to, shall, should, will, would.*. Explain that these are words that help other verbs in a present tense sentence. Model a few sentences for the students on the board:

1. I should invite Delia to the party.

2. I will blow up the balloons.

3. I must take the cake out of the oven.

Distribute Worksheet 20.4. Read the short story aloud. Encourage students to circle or underline any unfamiliar words in the text. Explain these words before students move on to the second part of the worksheet. Correct papers in class or collect and correct when the lesson is finished.

Worksheet 20.1: Language Blast

Irregular Past Tense Verbs

DIRECTIONS Imagine you had party at your house last weekend. Read each sentence that tells what happened. Then write the present form of each underlined past tense verb on the line. The first one is done for you.

1. I <u>felt</u> nervous before my guests arrived. I wanted everyone to have fun.
_____feel_____

2. Keisha arrived first. I <u>met</u> her at the door. _____

3. Ivan <u>brought</u> a fruit salad. _____

4. Danette <u>gave</u> me flowers. _____

5. While everyone talked, I <u>took</u> the chicken out of the oven. _____

6. This was the first time that Keisha and Ivan <u>met</u>. _____

7. I knew the party was going well when I <u>heard</u> people laughing. _____

8. After dinner, we <u>drank</u> milk and ate cookies outside. _____

9. We all gasped when we <u>saw</u> a shooting star. _____

10. I was very tired by the time everyone <u>went</u> home. _____

Worksheet 20.2: Vocabulary Development

How Do I Use My Utensils?

DIRECTIONS Use words from the word bank to complete each sentence. Some words are used more than once.

WORD BANK

plate	cup	napkin	spoon
knife	bowl	glass	fork

1. Mom put a piece of chicken on my _____.

2. I poured some water into my _____.

3. I used a _____ to eat my salad.

4. I placed my _____ on my lap.

5. Jamal asked if I wanted a _____ of coffee.

6. Suki used a _____ to cut the cake.

7. There was also a large _____ of fruit salad.

8. I ate my cake and fruit salad with my _____.

9. Then I wiped my face with my _____.

10. I helped wash my _____, _____, _____, _____,

_____, bowl, and _____.

Worksheet 20.3: Speaking and Listening

More Irregular Past Tense Verbs

DIRECTIONS Form pairs. The first student says each verb aloud. Then the second student writes the past tense form.

1. begin _____   2. send _____

3. fall _____   4. teach _____

5. forget _____   6. think _____

7. fly _____   8. throw _____

9. know _____   10. understand _____

11. make _____   12. win _____

13. pay _____   14. write _____

DIRECTIONS Complete each sentence by writing the correct verb tense of the word in parentheses.

15. Macsoud _____ his science project last night. (make)

16. Paulo _____ a poem last week. (write)

17. Fran _____ the ball to first base. (throw)

18. Charisse _____ to bring her lunch to school. (forget)

19. Fabian _____ the game for his team. (win)

20. Thomas _____ a letter to his grandma. (send)

Worksheet 20.4: Reading and Fluency

Word Choice

DIRECTIONS Read the story about a party.

Jena's Party

Jena is having a party so everyone can celebrate the end of the school year. First, she must send invitations to all her friends. Next, she should start planning the party. She would like to have balloons and flowers for decorations. She will go to the store with her mother to get some supplies. Her mother tells her that she ought to make party favors for her guests. "I think I shall make nametags for everyone," Jena tells her mom. On the day of the party, a few friends come early. They ask if they can help. Jena says they may blow up balloons. "You need to hurry! The rest of the guests will be arriving soon!" Mom says.

DIRECTIONS Then read each question. Circle the word you will use in your answer. Answer each question in a complete sentence.

1. Why is Jena having a party? (could/can)

_____

_____

2. What does Jena have to do first? (must/may)

_____

_____

3. What does Jena want to have at the party? (would/could)

_____

_____

4. What does Jena's mother tell her to do? (ought to/might)

_____

_____

5. What do Jena's friends ask her? (can/would)

_____

_____

6. What does Jena tell them? (might/may)

_____

_____

Worksheet 20.5: Daily Review

Throwing a Party

DIRECTIONS Pretend that you are having a party. In sentence 1, write the word that best completes each present tense sentence. Then write the past tense of each underlined verb in sentence 2 of each pair.

1. Present tense: I _____ (might/must) <u>send</u> out invitations.

   Past tense: I _____ out invitations.

2. Present tense: I think I _____ (shall/would) <u>make</u> party favors for all of my guests.

   Past tense: I _____ party favors for all of my guests.

3. Present tense: I _____ (would/should) <u>begin</u> decorating in the morning.

   Past tense: I _____ decorating in the morning.

4. Present tense: I _____ (ought to/can) <u>run</u> to the store before the guest arrive.

   Past tense: I _____ to the store before the guests arrived.

5. Present tense: I _____ (must/would) not <u>forget</u> to take the cake out of the oven.

   Past tense: I did not _____ to take the cake out of the oven.

Game 1: Memory Game

DIRECTIONS: Photocopy the table below (make 1-3 copies depending on class size) and cut out individual sentences. Make sure students feel comfortable pronouncing the vocabulary before starting.

Distribute the strips of paper so that everybody has one sentence. Start at one corner of the room, asking the student to read his or her sentence aloud to the class: "I am a girl." Now the teacher should repeat: "She is a girl." and then add his or her own sentence: "I am a teacher."

The teacher then invites the next student to follow the pattern: "She is a girl." "He is a teacher." "I am a teammate." This continues until every student has taken a turn. Anybody who needs more than one clue to complete his or her turn is out.

I am a student.	I am a girl.
I am a sister.	I am a boy.
I am a brother.	I am a cook.
I am a teammate.	I am a musician.
I am a coach.	I am an artist.
I am a friend.	I am an athlete.

Game 2: Bingo

DIRECTIONS: Photocopy the bingo cards and markers. Make sure students feel comfortable pronouncing the vocabulary before starting. Read the bingo clues aloud to students and have them choose the correct square to place their markers on.

CARD:

B	I	N	G	O
favorite book	state	phone number	city	favorite food
birth date	name	city	birth date	street
street	favorite movie	free space	state	name
city	favorite food	address	favorite book	address

MARKERS:

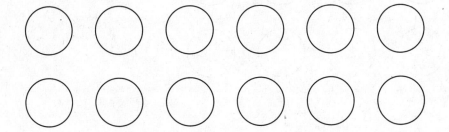

Game 2: Bingo

CARD:

B	I	N	G	O
state	address	birth date	city	phone number
city	phone number	free space	favorite movie	birth date
favorite book	street	favorite movie	name	state
favorite food	name	address	state	favorite food

MARKERS:

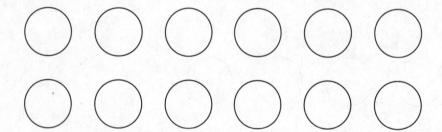

Game 2: Bingo Clues

Cities	States	Birth Dates	Addresses	Phone numbers	Books	Names	Foods	Movies
Chicago	Illinois	November 4, 1990	204 Main Street	(123) 567-7645	Junie B. James Books	George	Bananas	Bocky Movies
San Diego	California	April 1, 2000	3 Easy Avenue	(215) 547-6408	Harriet Potter Books	Katie	Spaghetti	Lord of the Ringers Movies
Spring-field	Missouri	May 6, 1993	4 Lowry Boulevard	(527) 765-6503	Harry and Mudge Books	Jed	Chocolate cake	Mission Possible Movies
Atlanta	Kentucky	March 20, 1999	99 Rolling Hills Lane	(219) 321-2378	Baby-sitters Club Books	Sarah	Steak	Harriet Potter Movies
Las Vegas	Georgia	June 24, 1995	456 State Road 57	(536) 640-3206	Magic School Bug Books	Mary	Corn on the cob	E.B. Movie

Game 3: Charades

DIRECTIONS: Photocopy and cut out individual phrases. Place the strips into a bag or cup. Make sure students feel comfortable pronouncing the vocabulary before starting.

Choose a student volunteer to pick out one of the phrases from the bag to act out. Ask the class: *What is (student) doing?* Have the class guess what the student is doing. Encourage students to use complete sentences. Have students take turns choosing a strip from the bag and acting out the phrases. To vary the verb forms, have two or three students act out the same phrase to practice plural forms.

going out	reading a book	singing a song	talking on the phone	watching a movie
listening to music	walking to school	eating a meal	playing a game	drinking a drink

Game 4: Comparison Game

DIRECTIONS: Photocopy the card and cut out the strips. Make sure students feel comfortable pronouncing the vocabulary before starting.

I am bigger than . . .	I am bigger than . . . I am the biggest.
I am taller than . . .	I am taller than . . . I am the tallest.
I am thinner than . . .	I am thinner than . . . I am the thinnest.
I am shorter than . . .	I am shorter than . . . I am the shortest.
I am older than . . .	I am older than . . . I am the oldest.
I am quieter than . . .	I am quieter than. . . I am the most quiet.

Game 5: What Am I?

intelligent	funny	talkative
nervous	energetic	hopeful
elegant	stylish	frightened
playful	loving	happy
interesting	upset	excited

Game 6: Optional Charades

DIRECTIONS: Photocopy the card and cut out each action. Make sure students feel comfortable pronouncing the vocabulary before starting.

clean the room	sweep the floor
take out the trash	make the bed
dust the furniture	vacuum the carpet
read	study/review
practice an instrument	play a sport

Game 7: What Time Is It?

DIRECTIONS: Cut the clock face and arms out. Then either laminate the clock or glue it onto a piece of cardboard. Affix the arms to the face of the clock using a tack pin.

Move the arms around the clock, and ask students: *What time is it?* Students must write the correct time on their papers. The first student(s) to get five correct answers wins.

Game 8: Party Matching Game

DIRECTIONS: Cut out the pictures and word cards shown below. Make sure students are comfortable with the vocabulary before beginning. Have students match each word with the correct object.

fork	knife	bowl
spoon	**plate**	**glass**

Lesson 1

Lesson 2

Worksheet 1.1: Language Blast
Cardinal Numbers

1. 19
2. 42
3. 1,903
4. eighty nine
5. three hundred thirteen
6. three thousand six hundred

Worksheet 1.2: Vocabulary Development
People We Know

1. musician
2. athlete
3. artist
4. cook
5. girls
6. boy
7. teammates
8. coach
9. friends

Worksheet 1.3: Speaking and Listening
Plural Nouns

1. athletes
2. teammates
3. musicians
4. coaches
5. artists
6. friends
7. cooks
8. teachers
9. girls
10. ladies
11. boys
12. babies

Dialogue
Answers will vary.

Worksheet 1.4: Reading and Fluency
Reading for Understanding

1. They are **not** brothers.
2. They are **not** teachers.
3. They are students. (circle)
4. They are **not** coaches.
5. They are friends. (circle)
6. They are in the same class. (circle)
7. Anita is a new student. (circle)

Worksheet 1.5: Daily Review
Who Are You?
Answers will vary.

Worksheet 2.1: Language Blast
Money Exercises

1. $ 1.25
2. $ .12
3. $26.00
4. $ 5.00
5. $ .75
6. $ .20

Worksheet 2.2: Vocabulary Development
Crossword Puzzle

1. address
2. state
3. street
4. city
5. favorite
6. name
7. birth date
8. phone number

Worksheet 2.3: Speaking and Listening
Classroom Survey
Answers will vary.

Worksheet 2.4: Reading and Fluency
Reading for Understanding

1. Anita is from Caracas.
2. Freddy is from Beijing.
3. Anita's phone number is (123) 456-7890.
4. Anita's address is 15 Maple Lane.
5. Freddy's favorite movie is Star Wars.
6. Yes, they become friends.
7. Tom, Freddy, and Anita are going to the movies.

Worksheet 2.5: Daily Review
Dialogue

1. name
2. address
3. city, state
4. phone number
5. birth date

Lesson 3

Worksheet 3.1: Language Blast
Seasons

snow with winter
rain with spring
wind with fall
sun with summer
flowers with spring
cold with winter
hot with summer
fallen leaves with fall

Worksheet 3.2: Vocabulary Development
Daily Routine

1.	get up	7.	play sports
2.	brush teeth	8.	go home
3.	eat breakfast	9.	do homework
4.	go to school	10.	eat dinner
5.	at school	11.	watch TV
6.	eat lunch	12.	go to sleep

Worksheet 3.3: Speaking and Listening
Class Survey
Answers will vary.

Worksheet 3.4: Reading and Fluency
Reading for Understanding

1. Tom has school at 8.
2. Freddy wakes up at 5:45.
3. Tom and Anita go to soccer practice after school.
4. Freddy practices his saxophone.
5. They do their homework together.

Worksheet 3.5: Daily Review
What Do You Do?

1.	wakes	8.	plays
2.	takes	9.	walk
3.	brushes	10.	practice
4.	eat	11.	do
5.	go	12.	eats
6.	eat	13.	watches
7.	play	14.	talk
		15.	sleep

Lesson 4

Worksheet 4.1: Language Blast
Days of the Week

1. Monday, Tuesday, Wednesday, Thursday, and Friday
2. Saturday and Sunday   8. Friday
3. Monday   9. Saturday
4. Friday   10. Answers will vary.
5. Tuesday
6. Saturday
7. Sunday

Worksheet 4.2: Vocabulary Development
Classroom Objects and Supplies

1.	notebooks	7.	board
2.	desk	8.	erasers
3.	computer	9.	ruler
4.	chair	10.	textbooks
5.	pencil	11.	clock
6.	paper		

Worksheet 4.3: Speaking and Listening
Matching

1. Yes, I pass tests.
2. Yes, I ask questions.
3. Yes, I solve problems.
4. Yes, I take notes.
5. No, I don't teach lessons.
6. Yes, I help classmates.
7. Yes, I finish homework.

Worksheet 4.4: Reading and Fluency
Reading for Understanding

1. F   4. T
2. T   5. F
3. F

Worksheet 4.5: Daily Review
Who Asks Each Question?

1. A, B   5. A, C
2. A, B, C   6. A, C
3. B   7. A, B
4. B   8. A, C

Lesson 5 | Lesson 6

Worksheet 5.1: Language Blast
Daily Routine

1. getting out of bed
2. brushing teeth
3. taking a shower
4. brushing hair
5. eating breakfast
6. going to school
7. eating lunch
8. going home
9. doing homework
10. eating dinner
11. watching TV
12. going to bed

Worksheet 5.2: Vocabulary Development
Vocabulary Match

1. go to the doctor
2. call for help
3. police officer
4. firefighter
5. nurse
6. hospital
7. bandage
8. fire
9. earthquake

Verbs: go to the doctor, call for help
Nouns: police officer, firefighter, nurse, hospital, bandage, fire, earthquake

Worksheet 5.3: Speaking and Listening
Emergency Plans

1. Fire – Call 911 for the firefighters.
2. Flood – Evacuate the building. Unplug electrical things.
3. Earthquake – Get under your desk.
4. Robbery – Call 911 for the police. Evacuate the building.
5. Bleeding arm – Use a bandage. Put pressure on the wound. Go to the hospital.
6. Car accident – Call 911 for the police. Call 911 for the paramedics.

Worksheet 5.4: Reading and Fluency
Reading for Understanding

1. B
2. A
3. B
4. A

Worksheet 5.5: Daily Review
Imperative Commands

1. I or F
2. I or F
3. E
4. B
5. A or C
6. A or C
7. D
8. H
9. G

Worksheet 6.1: Language Blast
Months of the Year

1. December
2. Answers will vary.
3. Answers will vary.
4. Answers will vary.
5. Answers will vary.
6. October
7. November
8. January
9. July
10. Answers will vary.
11. Answers will vary.
12. Answers will vary.
13. Answers will vary.
14. Answers will vary.

Worksheet 6.2: Vocabulary Development
Matching

1. F
2. I
3. D
4. C
5. A
6. B
7. G
8. E
9. H

Worksheet 6.3: Speaking and Listening
What Do You Like To Do?

Answers will vary.

Worksheet 6.4: Reading and Fluency
Reading for Understanding

1. James is listening to music.
2. True
3. Yolanda plays the bass.
4. James plays the guitar.
5. True
6. Yolanda has to be in class in 3 minutes.
7. Yolanda and James will meet after school
8. True

Worksheet 6.5: Daily Review
What Are They Doing?

1. They are playing a game.
2. What is the girl doing?
3. What are the people doing?
4. What is the boy doing?
5. She is singing a song.
6. What is the family doing?
7. They are walking to school.
8. What are the friends doing?
9. He is talking on the phone.

Lesson 7

Worksheet 7.1: Language Blast
Months of the Year/ Days of the Week

1. Thursday
2. March
3. January
4. June
5. Sunday
6. September
7. August
8. Wednesday
9. October
10. Monday
11. April
12. December

Worksheet 7.2: Vocabulary Development
Matching and Speaking

1. What
2. Where
3. Why
4. Why
5. Who
6. What
7. Where
8. Hw
9. Who
10. When
11-13. Answers will vary.

Worksheet 7.3: Speaking and Listening
What Are The Students Doing?

1. playing a game
2. reading a book
3. listening to music
4. singing a song
5. eating a meal
6. walking to school
7. going out
8. watching a movie
9. talking on the phone

Worksheet 7.4: Reading and Fluency
Reading for Understanding

1. A
2. B
3. A
4. B

Worksheet 7.5: Daily Review
What Are They Doing?

Answers may vary.

Lesson 8

Worksheet 8.1: Language Blast
Parts of the Body

Placement of labels should indicate understanding of words to describe parts of the body.

Worksheet 8.2: Vocabulary Development
Image & Word Match

1. language arts
2. math
3. physical education
4. chemistry
5. music
6. science
7. history

Worksheet 8.3: Speaking and Listening
Class Interviews

Answers will vary.

Worksheet 8.4: Reading and Fluency
Reading for Understanding

1. True
2. False
3. False
4. True
5. False
6. True

Worksheet 8.5: Daily Review
Crossword

1. feet
2. toes
3. legs
4. ears
5. fingers
6. mouth
7. neck
8. hands
9. teeth
10. chest
11. hair
12. stomach

Lesson 9

Worksheet 9.1: Language Blast
Ordinal Numbers
1. first
2. ninth
3. fourth
4. thirteenth
5. twenty-fifth

Worksheet 9.2: Vocabulary Development
Matching
1. big – small
2. clean – dirty
3. tall – short
4. fat – thin
5. ugly – pretty

Worksheet 9.3: Speaking and Listening
Cars, Cars, Cars
1. pretty
2. small
3. big
4. long
5. clean
6. dirty
7. Answers will vary.

Worksheet 9.4: Reading and Fluency
Reading for Understanding
1. better
2. flier
3. "Battle of the Bands"
4. $500.00
5. Saturday
6. work

Worksheet 9.5: Daily Review
Word Search
Students will complete the word search.

Lesson 10

Worksheet 10.1: Language Blast
Directions and Adjectives
1. Kendra
2. Kim
3. Lia
4. Samad
5. Tito, Ahab, Kim, Ho
6. Antonio, Carla, Eno, Peri
7. Answers will vary.
8. Sara
9. Answers will vary.
10. Peri

Worksheet 10.2: Vocabulary Development
Picture and Vocabulary Match
1. hallway
2. locker
3. cafeteria
4. gym
5. office
6. library
7. classroom

Worksheet 10.3: Speaking and Listening
Tell Me Something
Answers will vary.

Worksheet 10.4: Reading and Fluency
Reading for Understanding
1. A. T   B. T
2. A. T   B. F
3. A. F   B. T
4. A. T   B. F
5. A. F   B. T
6. A. T   B. T

Worksheet 10.5: Daily Review
More or Less?
1. smallest
2. shorter
3. tallest
4. biggest
5. bigger
6. closer
7. louder
8. cleaner
9. dirtiest
10. smaller

Lesson 11

Worksheet 11.1: Language Blast
Adjectives
Answers will vary.

Worksheet 11.2: Vocabulary Development
Tell Me More
1. funnier
2. more nervous
3. more talkative
4. more elegant
5. more interesting
6. the most intelligent
7. most playful
8. most stylish
9. more energetic

Worksheet 11.3: Speaking and Listening
My Family
1. Rosa
2. energetic
3. Charlie
4. talkative
5. Marco's parents
6. Marco's family
7. Rosa
8. a dog

Worksheet 11.4: Reading and Fluency
Reading for Understanding
1. Chu was frightened on the plane.
2. True
3. The scenery in Alaska is duller than the scenery in Mexico.
4. Anana's mother will be the saddest when they leave Mexico.
5. True

Worksheet 11.5: Daily Review
Weather
1. Yes, Rio de Janeiro is warmer than San Francisco.
2. Yes, San Francisco is cloudier than Rio de Janeiro.
3. Rio de Janeiro is windier than San Francisco.
4. Yes, Rio de Janeiro has more rain than San Francisco.
5. Yes, San Francisco is cooler at night than Rio de Janeiro.

Lesson 12

Worksheet 12.1: Language Blast
Word Search
Students will complete the word search.

Worksheet 12.2: Vocabulary Development
Places to Go
Answers will vary.

Worksheet 12.3: Speaking and Listening
What Are You Doing?
Answers will vary.

Worksheet 12.4: Reading and Fluency
Reading for Understanding
1. It is her favorite.
2. Mexico is warmer than Alaska.
3. french fries
4. malls and cafés
5. She thinks it is cold and dull.

Worksheet 12.5: Daily Review
Vacation
Answers will vary.

Lesson 13

Worksheet 13.1: Language Blast
Comparatives and Superlatives
Answers will vary.

Worksheet 13.2: Vocabulary Development
I Think I will…
Part 1
  1. C
  2. A
  3. D
  4. B
Part 2
Answers will vary.

Worksheet 13.3: Speaking and Listening
Using the Simple Future Form
  1A. are you doing
  1B. am going to see
  2A. I'll come
  2B. Are you going
  3A. I will; are you going
  3B. starts; let's meet
  4A. I'll

Worksheet 13.4: Reading and Fluency
Reading for Understanding
Underline the following:
  1. City Center
  2. 9:30
  3. eat lunch at
  4. best
  5. help our planet

Worksheet 13.5: Daily Review
Making Your Own Flier
Answers will vary.

Lesson 14

Worksheet 14.1: Language Blast
Prepositions of Place
Answers will vary.

Worksheet 14.2: Vocabulary Development
Matching
  1. E
  2. A
  3. B
  4. J
  5. C
  6. H
  7. I
  8. F
  9. G
  10. D

Worksheet 14.3: Speaking and Listening
Getting Around Town
Answers will vary.

Worksheet 14.4: Reading and Fluency
Reading for Understanding
  1. train station
  2. post office
  3. supermarket
  4. stadium
  5. hotel

Worksheet 14.5: Daily Review
Answers will vary.

Lesson 15

Worksheet 15.1: Language Blast
Prepositions of Place

1. in
2. in front of
3. beside
4. in front of
5. at
6. on

Worksheet 15.2: Vocabulary Development
Matching

1. I
2. E
3. J
4. G
5. C
6. H
7. A
8. B
9. D
10. F

Worksheet 15.3: Speaking and Listening
Present Continuous Verbs

1. I am cleaning the room.
2. You are sweeping the floor.
3. He is taking out the trash.
4. She is making the bed.
5. They are dusting the furniture.
6. He is vacuuming the carpet.
7. I am studying for a test.
8. We are reading a book.
9. They are practicing a sport.
10. You are playing an instrument.

Worksheet 15.4: Reading and Fluency
Reading for Understanding

1. False - You should start studying many days before the exam.
2. True
3. False - You should take breaks every hour.
4. False - Flashcards are very helpful.
5. True
6. True

Worksheet 15.5: Daily Review
My Chores

Answers will vary.

Lesson 16

Worksheet 16.1: Language Blast
Time (with *at*)

1. B
2. D
3. B
4. A
5. B
6. C
7. B
8. B

Worksheet 16.2: Vocabulary Development
Answer a Reporter's Questions

Answers will vary.

Worksheet 16.3: Speaking and Listening
My Favorite Day

Answers will vary.

Worksheet 16.4: Reading and Fluency
Reading for Understanding

1. Spring Fair is Saturday, March 1st.
2. Tickets go on sale on February 18th.
3. Student tickets cost $4.00.
4. The Three-legged race starts at 2:00PM.
5. The band will be playing near the flagpole.
6. Bingo starts at 6:00PM.
7. The fireworks will be on the football field.

Worksheet 16.5: Daily Review
Time

1. A
2. D
3. C
4. B
5. B

Lesson 17

Worksheet 17.1: Language Blast
Trouble

Answers will vary.

Worksheet 17.2: Vocabulary Development
Had To and *Needed To*

Answers will vary.

Worksheet 17.3: Speaking and Listening
Making Excuses

Answers will vary.

Worksheet 17.4: Reading and Fluency
Reading for Understanding

1. They had to stand in a doorway because it started to rain.
2. Chin missed the bus because he had to buy an apple for Kim.
3. Chin and Kim looked for a phone because they needed to call home.
4. Chin and Kim stopped looking for a phone because they had to find the puppy's owner.
5. Chin had to walk Kim home.

Worksheet 17.5: Daily Review
Following the Rules

Answers will vary.

Lesson 18

Worksheet 18.1: Language Blast
Irregular Verbs in the Past Tense

I – was
you (singular) – were
he/she/it – was
we – were
you (plural)– were
they – were

I – had
you (singular)– had
he/she/it – had
we – had
you – (plural) had
they – had

Worksheet 18.2: Vocabulary Development
I Like / I Do Not Like

1. broccoli, 2. fish, 3. apple
4. strawberry, 5. soup, 6. tea
7. onion, 8. tomato, 9. water
10. chicken, 11. pasta, 12. ham

Worksheet 18.3: Speaking and Listening
Classroom Cooking

1. grapes, 2. sandwich, 3. blueberries, 4. carrots, 5. meat, 6. cheese, 7. bread

Worksheet 18.4: Reading and Fluency
Reading for Understanding

1. T; 2. T; 3. F; 4. T; 5. T

Worksheet 18.5: Daily Review
Nouns and Verbs

1. I was; 2. you were; 3. he/she/it is; 4. they are
5. I have; 6. he/she/it has; 7. we have; 8. they have

1. We were cutting lettuce.
2. I had a ham and cheese sandwich for lunch.
3. They are baking fish.
4. You had meat for dinner.
5. She is washing grapes.

Lesson 19

Worksheet 19.1: Language Blast
Irregular Past Tense Verbs

1. drink
2. took
3. see
4. bought
5. went
6. met
7. read
8. get

Worksheet 19.2: Vocabulary Development
Today and Yesterday

1. went
2. saw
3. ate
4. brought
5. took
6. got
7. fell

Worksheet 19.3: Speaking and Listening
On the Weekend…

Answers will vary.

Worksheet 19.4: Reading and Fluency
Irregular Past Tense Verbs

1. Carlos's mother said that dogs made too much noise.
2. He didn't think it would be fun to have a fish.
3. Uncle Alex had a hamster.
4. Uncle Alex thought a hamster was a lot of fun.
5. Carlos wanted to know where he could get a hamster.

Worksheet 19.5: Daily Review
Irregular Past Tense Verbs

1. Correct
2. Incorrect. In 1999, my teacher first met her husband.
3. Incorrect. Yesterday I saw my friends at the park.
4. Correct
5. Correct
6. Incorrect. A few days ago, I brought the wrong book to school.

Lesson 20

Worksheet 20.1: Language Blast
Irregular Past Tense Verbs

1. feel
2. meet
3. brings
4. gives
5. take
6. meet
7. hear
8. drink
9. see
10. goes

Worksheet 20.2: Vocabulary Development
How Do I Use My Utensils?

1. plate
2. glass
3. fork
4. napkin
5. cup
6. knife
7. bowl
8. fork
9. napkin
10. plate, cup, fork, knife, glass, spoon

Worksheet 20.3: Speaking and Listening
More Irregular Past Tense Verbs

1. began
2. sent
3. fell
4. taught
5. forgot
6. thought
7. flew
8. threw
9. knew
10. understood
11. made
12. won
13. paid
14. wrote
15. made
16. wrote
17. threw
18. forgot
19. won
20. sent

Worksheet 20.4: Reading and Fluency
Word Choice

1. Jena is having a party so everyone can celebrate the end of the school year.
2. Jena must send invitations first.
3. Jena would like to have balloons and flowers at the party.
4. Jena's mother says she ought to make party favors.
5. Jena's friends ask if they can help.
6. Jena says they may blow up balloons.

Worksheet 20.5: Daily Review
Throwing a Party

1. might – sent
2. shall – made
3. should – began
4. can – ran
5. must – forget
